Guides to
Educational
Media

Guides to Educational Media

Margaret I. Rufsvold
and Carolyn Guss

Third Edition

Films
Filmstrips
Kinescopes
Phonodiscs
Phonotapes
Programed Instruction Materials
Slides
Transparencies
Videotapes

 American Library Association / Chicago 1971

International Standard Book Number 0-8389-0096-8 (1971)

Library of Congress Catalog Card Number 75-162469

Copyright © 1971 by the American Library Association

Printed in the United States of America

Contents

Preface   vii

Educational Media Catalogs and Lists
Generally Available   1

Professional Organizations in the
Educational Media Field   76

Periodicals in the Educational Media
Field—A Selected List   81

Educational Media Catalogs and Lists
Published since 1957 but
Unavailable in 1971   90

Index   95

Preface

This publication, now entitled *Guides to Educational Media,* is the third edition of the authors' *Guides to Newer Educational Media* published in 1961 and 1967. It is a guide to catalogs and lists, services of professional organizations, and specialized periodicals which systematically provide information on nonprint educational media. The 1961 edition was based upon the authors' April 20, 1960, report to the U.S. Office of Education, entitled *Sources of Information about Newer Educational Media for Elementary and Secondary Education* (1950–60). That report was the initial step of a larger study to determine a feasible method of establishing bibliographic control of educational audiovisual media. The project was supported by a contract between the U.S. Office of Education and Indiana University under Title VII B of the National Defense Education Act.

This edition identifies and describes 153 educational media catalogs and indexes, including those in the 1960 report and the 1961 and 1967 editions which are currently available and have been revised or published since 1959. It is comprehensive within its scope rather than selective. As in the case of the two earlier editions, no attempt was made to evaluate the catalogs or indexes, but criteria were established for inclusion. The catalogs or lists should be: (1) published between January 1, 1960, and February 1, 1971, (2) separate publications with a considerable portion devoted to providing information about nonprint educational media, (3) available on a national basis to anyone interested in obtaining them, (4) published in the United States, and (5) designed to inform potential users concerning the availability and educational utility of one or more types of educational media.

The term *educational media* as used in the two earlier editions designated instructional materials which require special equipment and physical facilities. These types of media have continued to be the basic concern in this edition, namely 16mm and 8mm (regular and super) films and film loops, 35mm filmstrips, 2″ x 2″ and 3¼″ x 4″ slides, videotapes and kinescopes, phonodiscs and phonotapes, programed and computer-assisted instructional materials, and transparencies. However, there is presently a discernible trend toward multimedia indexes which include not only the types of media mentioned above but also a variety of other types of educational resources both printed and non-printed: books, maps, charts, globes, opaque pictures, dioramas, exhibits, realia, games, field trips, simulated activities, equipment, and special facilities or installations. The authors have deliberately chosen to include such comprehensive indexes in this edition.

The main section of *Guides to Educational Media* provides descriptive annotations of items. Compilers or publishers of the catalogs and lists were asked by the authors to verify the data in the annotations and the current availability of the publications, and to add any additional information, such as forthcoming revisions. This same verification process was followed for the first and second editions.

In addition to the main section, three others sections provide further information concerning certain aspects of media availability and utility. The second section identifies and describes 10 media organizations. The third section identifies and briefly describes 36 media periodicals. (Periodicals and organizations outside the United States were excluded.) The fourth section lists 66 catalogs and indexes which were included in the 1960 report and the first two editions and which have not been superseded by revision since 1959 or are unavailable. It also lists those catalogs which have been identified since the 1967 edition and are currently unavailable. Copies of these publications may still be available in libraries.

Certain types of catalogs and lists have been excluded. These are: (1) the trade catalogs and promotional publications of producers/distributors which include only the materials produced and/or distributed by them; (2) catalogs of collections of audiovisual materials in universities, colleges, public libraries, and school systems; (3) catalogs of collections distributed by special interest groups such as denominational organizations; (4) catalogs from other countries and from international organizations not published in the United States; and (5) catalogs in preparation.

Some examples of valuable sources of media information excluded by the authors' criteria are: Stanford University's *Meyer Library Audio Catalog,* the 1971 edition of R. R. Bowker's *Audiovisual Market Place,* Fisher Publishing's *Educators Purchasing Master—Audiovisual,* Catharine Williams' *Sources of Teaching Materials,* and Mayfield Bray's *Ford Film Collection in the National Archives.*

Examples of publications which promise to be useful and which are scheduled for release in 1971 but were not available to the authors for inclusion in this publication are the Educational Information Services' *Education Information Collection* (EIC), a research and reference collection of information about educational technology; three lists of non-print materials for elementary schools—Eugene Friese's *Audiovisual Resources for Grades K–8* (tentative title) and Ellin Greene and Madalynne Schoenfeld's *A Multi-Media Approach to Children's Literature,* both to

this is out 11/14/72

be published by the American Library Association, and R. R. Bowker's *Resources for Learning*; also from Bowker, Harry Johnson's *Multimedia* Materials for Afro-American Studies; and Bro-Dart's *The College Film Library Collection*, edited by Emily S. Jones. The National Information Center for Educational Media (NICEM) has announced that it is preparing, and will publish, several additional catalogs: *Index to Educational Audio Tapes, Index to Educational Video Tapes, Index to Educational Records, Index to Producers and Distributors, Index to Ecology,* and *Index to Black History and Studies.*

The authors of this publication are aware that some other useful lists are being published too late to be included. They feel, too, that others may have been omitted inadvertently. Because of a continuing interest in sources of information about the availability and utility of educational media, they welcome suggestions and announcements concerning relevant publications.

Throughout the work on this publication the authors have enjoyed the fullest cooperation of their colleagues at Indiana University and in other universities and educational organizations. They wish to acknowledge this help and to express their gratitude.

MARGARET I. RUFSVOLD, *Professor of Library Science*
Graduate Library School, Indiana University

CAROLYN GUSS, *Professor of Education and Associate in Selection*
Audio-Visual Center, Indiana University

Educational Media Catalogs and Lists Generally Available

1. **ABA Film Guide.** Public Relations Department, The American Bankers Association, 1120 Connecticut Ave., N.W., Washington, D.C. 20036. 1967. Free. 51p. (Revision scheduled for March 1971)
   Scope: Approximately 235 films and filmstrips about banking and related subjects. Materials described are not necessarily recommended for use by the ABA. Items produced by ABA are listed separately. Categories are: ABA films; ABA filmstrips; American Institute of Banking filmstrips; automation and data processing; commercial banking; credit; economics, business, and industry; Federal Reserve Bank films; Federal Reserve Bank filmstrips; financial planning, budgeting, and saving; investment banking and the stock market; money; public relations and related subjects; training films.
   Arrangement: Alphabetical by subject.
   Entries: Title, distributor, type of medium, running time, sound or silent, color or black and white,* purchase price, rental price, suggested audience, 30–100-word descriptive annotation.
   Special Features: Subject index; free-loan source; title index; list of points to remember before film showing.

2. **African Encounter: A Selected Bibliography of Books, Films, and Other Materials for Promoting an Understanding of Africa among Young Adults,** prepared by a committee of the Young Adult Services Division of the American Library Association. American Library Association, 50 E. Huron St., Chicago, Ill. 60611. 1963. $1.50. 69p.
   Scope: 45 films and filmstrips on Africa recommended primarily for young adults and any person between the ages of 13 and 19 or classes from the eighth grade through high school. Classified by the following subject headings: Africa (general), Central Africa, East Africa, West Africa, and South Africa.

*Hereafter *b/w* will be used instead of "black and white."

Arrangement: By medium (films and filmstrips) and then alphabetical by title under subject headings which are alphabetical.

Entries: Title, producer, production date, length or frames, color or b/w, purchase price or free loan, grade level.

Special Features: Foreword by G. Mennen Williams; bibliography of professional-level references for group leaders; suggestions for planning programs; organizations dealing with Africa; organizations including Africa in their programs; African embassies.

3. **African Film Bibliography 1965,** arranged by Warren D. Stevens in cooperation with the Educational Media Council. Committee on Fine Arts and the Humanities, African Studies Association, Indiana University, Bloomington, Ind. 47401. 1966. Apply. 31p. (Occasional Papers no.1)

Scope: Based on the listings in the *Educational Media Index,* the 311 films about sub-Saharan Africa are arranged under 79 subject headings, such as Africa—description and travel, art, children in Africa, colonialism, evangelistic work, music, Nile River, tropical diseases, wildlife, names of individuals, countries, and national parks.

Arrangement: Classified by subject. Most of the subject headings are geographical designations. Title index.

Entries: Title, source, date, size(mm), sound or silent, color or b/w, running time, age levels, price of rental or purchase, guide if available, 10–60-word descriptive annotation.

Special Features: List of subject headings; films on Africa no longer available; sources of films.

4. **American Film Festival Guide.** Educational Film Library Association, Inc., 17 W. Sixtieth St., New York, N.Y. 10023. Annual. 1959–67, $1. 1968–71. $2. Each volume paged separately. *Cumulative Index* 1959–63. 50c. 16 p. *American Film Festival Guides* 1959–63 (in pressboard binder with index), $5.

Scope: Descriptions of 16mm and 8mm films and 35mm filmstrips shown at the annual EFLA* American Film Festival. Films are classified under 44 comprehensive subject categories, such as agriculture, forestry, and natural resources; classroom films for lower grades; sculpture, architecture, and crafts. Filmstrips are classified by the following subject headings: science and math, social studies, geography, history, and economics. All films were preselected for showing at the festivals by local subject-category preview committees. More than 400 entries, about two-thirds of which are films.

Arrangement: Alphabetical by title within broad subject headings.

*EFLA, an acronym for Educational Film Library Association, Inc., is used throughout this guide instead of the full name of the Association.

Title index to page number and subject-category code number. Cumulative title index to year and page number in guides for 1959–63.

Entries: Title, series title if a filmstrip, series and number of filmstrips in series, color or b/w, running time or number of frames, silent or sound if a filmstrip, purchase price, producer, distributor, and mailing address. Brief annotation gives statement of the purpose, the recommended audience, and in about 25 words the content of each film and filmstrip.

5. **American Film Review: Films of America.** v.9. The American Educational and Historical Film Center, Eastern Baptist College, St. Davids, Pa. 19087. n.d. Free. 31p.

Scope: Motion pictures endorsed and approved by the American Educational and Historical Film Center; selected by "a distinguished committee of evaluators who personally reviewed the films not only for technical skills, but also for accuracy of content and freedom from subversive bias." The films fall into 5 broad categories of history: arts and letters, leaders, the enterprise system, the revolution, and the Communist challenge. More than 100 titles.

Arrangement: Alphabetical by title under broad categories. No index. Table of contents by broad categories.

Entries: Title, producer, distributor, color or b/w, running time, audience by grade level. Descriptive annotation of 10–25 words in 1–3 sentences, with specific content notes where necessary.

Special Features: Directories of film producers and distributors; trustees and officers of the Center; and members of the film selection committee.

6. **American Indians—An Annotated Bibliography of Selected Library Resources.** University of Minnesota, Library Services Institute for Minnesota Indians, Minneapolis, Minn. 55455. 1970. Apply. 156p.

Scope: Approximately 200 films, filmstrips, recordings, and slides on American Indians. Selected on the basis of 16 evaluative criteria by a 1969–70 institute funded by Title II, part B, of the 1965 Higher Education Act. Books also included.

Arrangement: Alphabetical by title under medium in two sections, "recommended" and "not recommended."

Entries: Title, length, rpm for records, color or b/w, sound or silent, producer, date, grade level, rental sources, rental rate, 50–100-word description of content.

7. **An Annotated Bibliography of Audiovisual Materials Related to Understanding and Teaching the Culturally Disadvantaged,** prepared by Lillian Dimitroff, Chicago State College, West Center. Available from Publications-Sales Section, National Education Association, 1201

Sixteenth St., N.W., Washington, D.C. 20036. 1969. 75c. 42p. Apply for discounts available on quantity orders.

Scope: Approximately 130 films and filmstrips and 12 records concerning appreciation and understanding of the culturally disadvantaged and 10 films and filmstrips on teaching the culturally disadvantaged. No effort was made to evaluate or select materials but the description of each item is intended to aid the user in selecting suitable material.

Arrangement: Alphabetical by medium under two headings, understanding culturally disadvantaged and teaching culturally disadvantaged.

Entries: Title, distributor, date, running time, color or b/w, number of phonodiscs, speed, size in diameter, purchase price, 30–100-word descriptive annotation.

Special Features: Distributor index.

8. **Annotated Bibliography of Films in Automation, Data Processing, and Computer Science,** by Martin B. Solomon, Jr., and Nora Geraldine Lovan. University of Kentucky Press, Lexington, Ky. 40506. June 1967. $3. 38p.

Scope: 244 films on automation, data processing, computer science, and related subjects.

Arrangement: 3 sections—title index, subject index, and annotated bibliography. Title index gives code number for each film in annotated bibliography. Subject index uses keywords to depict content of film and also has code number for annotated bibliography.

Entries: Film code, title, producer, distributor, date, running time, sound or silent, color or b/w, projector size, suggested audience, 30–50-word descriptive annotation, ordering information for borrowing films.

Special Features: Title index; subject index; directory of film depositories; instructions on how to use title and subject index in conjunction with annotated bibliography.

9. **An Annotated Bibliography of Integrated FLES Teaching Materials,** compiled by Helen B. Miller. Edited by Lorraine A. Strasheim. The Indiana Language Program, 101 Lindley Hall, Indiana University, Bloomington, Ind. 47401. 1969. 91p. Single copies free. Apply for quantity prices.

Scope: 11 French, 5 German, and 15 Spanish programs for elementary schools. Compiled to: assist foreign-language specialists, administrators, and teachers in the selection of materials best suited for them; inform all persons interested in Foreign Languages in the Elementary Schools (FLES) of the scope and availability of planned programs; and encourage FLES teachers to use the commercial programs available.

Programs selected can be used in a continuing program for at least 2 years. Programs were selected by a committee of individuals who have recently been connected with FLES.

Arrangement: Alphabetical by producer under foreign language.

Entries: Title, publisher, type of medium, time allotment, teacher training requirements, methods, content, teacher's manual, student book, articulation of this program with next levels, general comments.

Special Features: Description of how the committee completed this project, including evaluation forms; FLES materials list; minimal objectives for modern foreign-language teachers; description of Indiana Language Program.

10. **Annotated Bibliography on the Professional Education of Teachers.** The Association for Student Teaching, a department of National Education Association, Richard E. Collier, executive secretary. Available from Publications-Sales Section, National Education Association, 1201 Sixteenth St., N.W., Washington, D.C. 20036. 1969. $1.75. 175p. (Stock no.861−24476) Apply for quantity discounts.

Scope: Divided into 2 sections. Section 1 deals with literature on professional education. Section 2 deals with nonprint materials for the professional sequence and includes approximately 175 titles including films, filmstrips, phonodiscs, and phonotapes. All listings are from commercial and noncommercial catalogs published in 1967 and 1968 and are intended for use in methods courses and curriculum media libraries. Subject areas include: general curriculum organization and assessment of instruction, characteristics of pupils, relationships between teaching and learning, study of teachers and teaching, teaching in different subject areas and grade levels, teaching the disadvantaged and atypical pupil, and production of materials and use of new media.

Arrangement: Alphabetical by subject area and then alphabetical by title.

Entries: Title, producer, distributor, type of medium, running time, color or b/w, purchase price, 20–100-word descriptive annotation.

Special Features: Source index; publication list and order blank.

11. **An Annotated List of Recordings in the Language Arts,** compiled and edited by Morris Schreiber. National Council of Teachers of English, 508 S. Sixth St., Champaign, Ill. 61820. 1964. $1.75. 83p. (Stock no.47906) (Supplement scheduled for 1971)

Scope: An annotated selected list of phonorecords to aid English teachers in elementary schools, secondary schools, and colleges. Categories and subjects include: American literature as well as folk literature, American history, world history and social studies, English and American poetry and prose, drama and Shakespeare, documentaries, lectures and speeches, and anthologies. 436 entries.

Arrangement: The annotated list is divided into 3 sections—recordings for elementary schools, recordings for secondary schools, and recordings for college classes—arranged by type or form; separate table of contents for each section; title and author indexes.

Entries: Title or album title, producer or distributor, author, reader or performers, number of phonodiscs, order number, rpm, price, 20–60-word descriptive annotation.

Special Features: List of recording companies, distributors, sales agents; spiral binding.

12. Audio Cardalog, edited by Max U. Bildersee. Box 989, Larchmont, N.Y. 10538. 1958–1969. $30 per year. Suspended publication in 1970. Limited supply of v.6 (1962) through v.12 (1969) available.

Scope: Reviews of phonodiscs and phonotapes on cards including productions of major as well as minor phonodisc and phonotape producers. Designed for schools, colleges, libraries, and instructional materials centers and providing full data for use of administrators, supervisors, curriculum specialists, teachers, and students. At least 400 cross-indexed 3″ x 5″ cards each year in 10 issues.

Arrangement: Cards come in sets and may be arranged alphabetically by author, title, subject, or curriculum area, as best suited to local use.

Entries: Title, phonorecord label, number of discs, speed (either rpm or ips), size in diameter, credits, *Audio Cardalog* number, subject headings and added entries suggested, general rating, interest level and utilization, critical/evaluative annotation of about 25 words, descriptive annotation of 25–50 words giving synopsis of phonorecord.

Special Features: Each card punched and ready for interfiling into an already existing card catalog; periodic alphabetical indexing and subscriber's advisory service.

13. Audio-Visual Aids for Data Processing Systems. Data Processing Management Association, International Headquarters, 505 Busse Highway, Park Ridge, Ill. 60068. 1966. 50c. 20p.

Scope: Approximately 100 films dealing with data processing, systems, automation, process charts, and work simplification.

Arrangement: Alphabetical by title.

Entries: Title, 75–150-word description of content, 16mm, sound or silent, color or b/w, rental, code number of source for ordering film.

Special Features: Addresses of rental sources; alphabetical title index.

14. **Audio-Visual Guidance Materials: An Annotated Bibliography and Directory of Minnesota Sources,** prepared by Truly Trousdale Latchaw. State Department of Education, St. Paul, Minn. 55101. Available from Documents Section, State Department of Education, 140 Centennial Bldg., St. Paul, Minn. 55101. 1970. $3.45. 484p.
    Scope: Includes approximately 1,600 titles of 16mm motion pictures, filmstrips, and phonotapes related to the field of guidance and available from 1 or more of the 34 identified sources in Minnesota. The subject is divided into 5 major areas: family life, personal–social development, careers, personal–social problems, and education.
    Arrangement: Divided into two main sections—functional index and an alphabetical listing, which is the main entry section. The functional index is an alphabetical list of titles in 3 parts: films (16mm), filmstrips, and tapes. Information concerning age group, subject, EFLA evaluation, and page number of main entry are given for each title. The alphabetical listing is divided into 3 parts—part 1, films (16mm); part 2, filmstrips; part 3, tapes. Each part is arranged first by grade level, then by subject, then alphabetically by title.
    Entries: Main entries are in the section entitled "Alphabetical Listing" and include: title, producer, date, screening time, silent or sound, color or b/w, number of frames or number of filmstrips in a series, running time of tapes, EFLA evaluation when available, level, subject area, descriptive annotation in 20–100 words, and availability information concerning loan, rental, or purchase.
    Special Features: An introduction to the use of films entitled "The Classroom Film in Guidance and Counselling," by Arnold Luce; Minnesota audiovisual sources; rules and procedures for borrowing audiovisual materials from selected sources.

15. **An Audio Visual Guide to Shakespeare.** Educational Film Library Association, Inc., 17 W. Sixtieth St., New York, N.Y. 10023. 1962. 75c. 8p. (EFLA Service Supplement) (Revision scheduled for 1971)
    Scope: Audiovisual materials on and about Shakespeare, including biography and background, theater, plays, anthologies, poetry, and analysis. The types of media are 16mm films, 35mm filmstrips, 33⅓ rpm phonodiscs, and phonotapes on deposit at the National Tape Repository. More than 250 entries.
    Arrangement: By subject—alphabetical by title under medium.
    Entries: Title or series title, producer/distributor, running time, date, color or b/w, sound or silent, number of frames if a filmstrip,

phonodisc number, a brief statement of content.
Special Features: Directory of sources.

16. **Audio Visual Materials for Teaching about Communism.** Educational Film Library Association, Inc., 17 W. Sixtieth St., New York, N.Y. 10023. 1962. 75c. 4p. (EFLA Service Supplement) (Revision scheduled for 1971)

    Scope: Selected motion pictures and filmstrips which can be used in teaching about communism and are recommended as better than average in technical quality. As far as possible, the materials appear to be fair-minded and factual, although they may be biased to some degree. The list is divided into 6 broad categories: history of the Soviet Union, Communist doctrine, life in the Soviet Union today, Russia's satellites, communism and Germany, and Communist China. 47 titles.

    Arrangement: Alphabetical by title under subject categories. No index.

    Entries: Title, producer, distributor, running time or number of frames, sound or silent if a filmstrip, color or b/w, date, brief descriptive annotation of 10–25 words, audience level, EFLA rating if reviewed by an EFLA evaluating committee.

    Special Features: Directory of sources.

17. **Audiovisual Materials in Dentistry.** American Dental Association, Bureau of Audiovisual Service, 211 E. Chicago Ave., Chicago, Ill. 60611. 1970. Free. 101p.

    Scope: Films on all phases of dentistry, including dental technical (for professional audiences) and dental health (for nonprofessional audiences). A listing of films available for rental and loan from the American Dental Association Film Library. Approximately 400 16mm film, filmstrip, and slide titles are listed.

    Arrangement: By subject with subject and title indexes.

    Entries: Title, distributor or producer, running time, sound or silent, color or b/w, audience suitability, date of release, rental and purchase source. Where the source is American Dental Association, the cost is given. Descriptive annotation of 20–50 words, series notes, some program suggestions.

    Special Features: Sources for films and filmstrips; television clearance information; some utilization suggestions.

18. **Audio-Visual Resource Guide.** 8th ed. National Council of the Churches of Christ in the U.S.A. Available from Department of Publication Services, National Council of Churches, 475 Riverside Dr., New York, N.Y. 10027. 1966. $3.95. 597p. (9th ed. scheduled for publication late in 1971)

    Scope: More than 3,800 films, filmstrips, phonodiscs, phonotapes, slides, and other types of graphic materials dealing with such church-related subject areas as: international social order, personal Christian living, the Bible, God, the family, domestic social order, learning process, instructional media, instructional techniques, the United Nations, the Christian church, biographies of great missionaries, mental health, physical health, sex education, alcohol, narcotics, housing, war and peace, and civil liberties.

Arrangement: Alphabetical by title.

Entries: Title, number in series, length, type of medium, color or b/w if film or filmstrip, size and speed if phonodisc or phonotape, guide (if available), producer, date of production, distributor, sale and/or rental rate, 75–200-word description of content, 75–200-word evaluation critique, recommendation (highly recommended, recommended, acceptable, limited, not recommended, on the basis of evaluations prepared by leaders in Christian education meetings in 50 interdenominational committees throughout the United States), principal teaching purpose, and code for recommended audience (N, nursery—up to 3 years; K, kindergarten—ages 4 and 5; PRI, primary—grades 1 and 2; LJ, lower junior—grades 3 and 4; J, junior—grades 5 and 6; JH, junior high—grades 7, 8, and 9; SH, senior high —grades 10, 11, and 12; YP, young people—ages 18 to 23; YA, young adults—ages 24 to 40; A, adults—over 40; PAR, parents; L-T, leaders and teachers; FAM, family), subject heading codes referring to the specific subject heading(s) under which the unit is listed in the subject heading index.

Special Features: Subject-heading index with titles listed alphabetically; distributor index; list of materials evaluated in the seventh edition of the *Guide* (AVRG) and deleted in the eighth; bibliography of books and periodicals in the communication field; 10 pages for notes; detachable order cards for *AVRG* and *Associates Quarterly.*

19. **Audiovisual Resources for Teaching Instructional Technology: An Annotated Listing.** 3d ed. Area of Instructional Technology, Syracuse University, 123 College Place, Syracuse, N.Y. 13210. 1971. $3.60. 164p.

Scope: Approximately 800 titles. A comprehensive listing of audiovisual materials related to the activities of instructional materials coordinators, consultants, instructors in instructional technology programs, audiovisual specialists, librarians, and students. Subject areas include: administration; facilities; instructional design; learning and communications; media equipment; media production; media utilization; research; instructional techniques; and society, education, and technology.

Arrangement: Alphabetical by title within subject headings.

Entries: Title, 30–50-word descriptive annotation, producer, date,

type of medium, sound or silent, color or b/w, sale price and/
or rental price.

Special Features: Producer code index; series index; title index.

20. **The Black Man in Films—African Heritage and American History,**
    compiled by Arthur S. Meyers. Enoch Pratt Free Library, 400 Cathe-
    dral St., Baltimore, Md. 21201. 1969. 10c. 12p. 1971 *Supplement.* 10c.
    7p.

    Scope: 73 films and filmstrips on or about the black man in general
      and on such specific subjects as: the arts, Africa, growing up
      black, confrontation.

    Arrangement: Alphabetical by subject areas and then alphabetical
      by title.

    Entries: Title, color (only when film or filmstrip is not b/w), filmstrip
      or filmstrip and recording (only when the title is not a film)
      length, 50–100-word description of content.

    Special Features: Directions for borrowing from Pratt Library agen-
      cies and from other local and county libraries.

21. **The Black Record: A Selective Discography of Afro-America on
    Audio Discs.** Washington University Libraries, Audio-Visual Depart-
    ment, St. Louis, Mo. 63130. 1969 with April 1970 *Supplement.* 50c
    prepaid; $1.50 if billing required. 13p.

    Scope: More than 100 phonodiscs dealing with black history. Docu-
      mentary and spoken word recording classifications include
      biographical material, speeches, poetry, prose, and drama.
      Included are such persons as W. E. B. Du Bois, Frederick
      Douglass, Booker T. Washington, Malcolm X, Martin Luther
      King, Jr., and Stokely Carmichael. Folk music classifications
      include rhythm and blues, game songs, ballads, hollers and
      shouts, spirituals and gospel songs, work songs and calls.
      Emphasis is placed on "authentic" folk recordings and they
      range from origins in Africa to "Songs of the Selma-Mont-
      gomery March."

    Arrangement: Divided into 2 major sections—section 1, documen-
      tary and spoken word, and section 2, folk music. Each section
      alphabetical by title, author, or artist.

    Entries: Local call number, title and author/artist or author/artist
      and title, 10–15-word description of content or list of contrib-
      utors, producer/phonorecord number.

    Special Features: Addresses of phonorecord manufacturers and
      distributors.

    Authors' Note: All the recordings in this listing are in the John M.
      Olin Library, Washington University, which has been conscien-
      tiously attempting to build a complete collection of commer-
      cially available phonodiscs dealing with black history. The list

is intended not only as a local-use reference tool but also as a purchase guide on a wider basis.

22. **Blue Book of Audiovisual Materials.** 45th ed. Educational Screen and Audiovisual Guide, 434 S. Wabash Ave., Chicago, Ill. 60605. 1970. $2. 62p. Annual, in July/August issue of *Educational Screen AV Guide.*

Scope: Motion pictures, filmstrips, slides, phonodiscs, and phonotapes in 33 subject fields for use by teachers of all grade levels. Approximately 1,200 titles produced in the 12 months preceding publication. Subjects include: art, cinema, education, entertainment, environment, foreign languages, geography, guidance and human relations, health and safety, history, language arts, literature, mathematics, music, physical education, primary, religion, science, sex education, social studies, and vocational education.

Arrangement: Alphabetical by subject and then alphabatical by title.

Entries: Title, type of material, running time or number of frames or slides, silent or sound, color or b/w, cost for purchase and/or rental of motion pictures and filmstrips, speed (rpm) and size in diameter of phonodiscs, interest level, availability of teachers' guides or manuals, descriptive annotation in 10–50 words, Reader's Service Number coded to all producers/distributors.

Special Features: Title index; two Readers' Service Number cards which include numbers for all producers and distributors to enable readers to channel requests for information concerning items through *Educational Screen Audiovisual Guide.*

23. **Boating Films Directory,** compiled by the National Association of Engine and Boat Manufacturers, Inc., 537 Steamboat Rd., Greenwich, Conn. 06830. 1970. Free. 54p.

Scope: Motion pictures on recreational boating and related subjects. Free and sponsored. Approximately 400 listings in 14 sections.

Arrangement: Classified by subject, such as construction, cruising and camping, fishing, motorboat racing, navigation, safety and maintenance, sailing, technical, water sports, and weather. Title index.

Entries: Title, distributor, running time, silent or sound, color or b/w, descriptive annotation of 10–25 words, symbol indicating clearance for television.

Special Features: Directory of sources; how to obtain films.

24. **Catalog of Audio-Visual Aids for Counselor Training in Mental Retardation and Emotional Disability, v.1; Films,** prepared by Devereux Foundation Institute for Research and Training. The Devereux Foundation, Devon, Pa. 19333. 1967. Free. 104p.

Scope: Approximately 350 films selected for use in university coun-
selor-training programs and in agency in-service training
programs preparing staff for work with the mentally and emotionally handicapped. Subject areas include: aggression,
aphasia, autism, community service, counseling, day hospitals,
defense mechanisms, depression, drugs, emotional disability,
epilepsy, evaluation techniques, frustration, hypnosis, juvenile
delinquency, learning difficulties, mental hygiene, mental illness, mental retardation, neurology, occupational therapy,
schizophrenia, senility, sheltered workshop, speech therapy,
stress, suicide, and therapy.
Arrangement: Alphabetical by subject and then alphabetical by title.
Entries: Title, running time, color or b/w, 10–50-word descriptive
annotation, distributor code, date if available.
Special Features: Subject index; state and territorial mental health
authorities listing; distributor index.

25. **Catalog of Captioned Films for the Deaf,** prepared by Anita A.
Carpenter. Division of Educational Services, Bureau of Education
for the Handicapped, Office of Education, U.S. Department of Health,
Education and Welfare, Washington, D.C. 20202. 1967. Apply. 102p.
Scope: Captioned motion pictures of general interest in broad categories, such as adventure and action, biographical drama,
comedy, documentary, drama, driver education, guidance, fan-
tasy, mystery, sports, western, and science fiction; classroom
films for instructional areas, such as business and economics,
language arts, literature, science, and social studies; and films
and filmstrips for teacher education. Available to all registered
schools and classes for the deaf. More than 500 entries.
Arrangement: In 3 main sections—general interest films, alphabetical
by title; classroom films for instructional purposes, alphabetical by title; teacher training films and filmstrips, by topic.
Subject index.
Entries: Title, performers, running time, color or b/w, interest level,
subject area, code designating suitability for general audience
or adults only, 20–100-word descriptive annotation.
Special Features: Distributing centers; overview of the captioned
films for the deaf program; list of films withdrawn from cir-
culation.

26. **Catalog of Recorded Instruction for Television.** Great Plains National Instructional Television Library, University of Nebraska, Lincoln, Neb. 68508. 1971. Free. 136p.
Scope: Approximately 100 complete telecourses on the elementary,
junior high, senior high, college and adult levels in such subject areas as: business, driver education, drug education,
communications, education, fine arts, foreign languages, geog-

raphy, history, humanities, journalism, language arts, mathematics, nursing education, philosophy, psychology, science, social science, sociology, vocational education.

Arrangement: Divided into 3 sections according to grade level—elementary and junior high school, secondary, and adult levels and college. At least 1 full page is devoted to each telecourse.

Entries: Title, number and length of lessons, specific grade level, approximately one-half page description of content, photograph of television teacher or comparable illustration, producer.

Special Features: Photographs of Great Plains staff, policy board, and engineers; general information including pricing structure, definitions of specialized terms, conditions of use, descriptions of supplementary materials; library history and listing of users.

27. **CINE/70 Golden Eagle Film Awards.** Council on International Nontheatrical Events, 1201 Sixteenth St., N.W., Washington, D.C. 20036. 1970. $2. 64p. Published annually since 1958.

Scope: Approximately 200 CINE Golden Eagle films produced in 1969 and selected in 1970 by CINE evaluating procedures, in accordance with regulations specified on page 43 of this yearbook, from among more than 650 entries from the United States as outstanding examples of film productions in such areas as: agriculture, animation, architecture, amateur adult, amateur youth, the arts, business and industry, education, experimental / avant-garde, history-anthropology-archeology, maritime, medical, public health, safety, science and technology, social documentary and religion, sports, theatrical short subjects, travel and tourism—exploration, and television and short documentary. Evaluative criteria recommended by CINE for use by evaluators in rating films include: imagination, creativeness, and cinematographic excellence; authenticity, honesty, and sensitivity; presentation of the United States, other countries, their people and institutions, in a fair and objective manner; brevity in telling point; experimental and unique approaches; ability to be understood by a variety of international audiences or by specialized international audiences; new insights into the subject, imparting a sense of revelation; and visual imagery, with image and sound in artistic unity.

Arrangement: Alphabetical by title.

Entries: Title, length; color or b/w; sponsor; producer; production credits including names of such staff as director, editor, cameraman, composer, narrator, sound technician, art and animation technicians, etc.; 20–60-word descriptions of content; Library of Congress card number.

Special Features: Introduction by CINE President William G. Carr; explanation of CINE's role, sponsors and awards system and ceremonies; CINE patrons; CINE international honors; CINE Eagle films produced by adult amateurs; 1970 international calendar of festivals in which American films were entered through CINE; instructions and requirements for submitting films to CINE; CINE jurors; list of producers, sponsors, and distributors; CINE international outreach, officers, and directors.

28. **Civil Rights: A Selected List of Films, Filmstrips, and Recordings.** Educational Film Library Association, Inc., 17 W. Sixtieth St., New York, N.Y. 10023. 1964. $1. 6p. (EFLA Service Supplement) (Revision scheduled for 1971)

Scope: Includes media concerned with the historical background of civil rights as well as contemporary movements; for example, the Bill of Rights, racial discrimination, suffrage, Susan B. Anthony, constitutional amendments, employment, education, voting, and public accommodations. More than 100 entries.

Arrangement: Alphabetical by broad subject areas, then by type of medium and under medium, alphabetical by title.

Entries: Title or series title, producer/distributor, date, mm, rpm, ips, track, number of frames if a filmstrip, color or b/w, running time, phonodisc size and number, brief descriptive annotation.

Special Features: Directory of sources.

29. **The Civil War in Motion Pictures, A Bibliography of Films Produced in the United States since 1897,** compiled by Paul C. Spehr, Library of Congress. Available from Superintendent of Documents, U.S. Government Printing Office, Washington, D.C. 20025. 1961. 60c. 109p.

Scope: 868 films and filmstrips depicting, through fact or fiction, events of the period 1855–70, the immediate causes of the Civil War, the war itself, and its aftermath in the Reconstruction period. Of the motion pictures produced for television, only those released for educational distribution, apart from commercial television broadcasting, have been included. A special section listing newsreels is included. Many of the films were produced before 1915 and are not currently available.

Arrangement: Alphabetical by title.

Entries: Title, producer, distributor, date, running time, sound or silent, color or b/w, 20–65-word descriptive annotation, credits, when available.

Special Features: List of principal sources; combined title index and subject index; index of literary works upon which titles are based.

30. **Development and Structure of Industry—Instructional Aids List and Bibliography.** College of Industry, Wisconsin State University, Platteville, Wis. 53818. 1970. $6.50. (Price includes 3 related publications —*Study Guide, Information and Job Sheets,* and *Teaching Plan.*) 50p.

Scope: Includes 84 films, 10 filmstrip series, 9 individual filmstrips, 4 videotapes, 13 charts, 43 multimedia kits, 2 games, and 54 books and pamphlets. The listing is not considered exhaustive or complete. It is considered "broad enough in scope to enable the instructor to teach the development and scope of industry."

Arrangement: Media are grouped according to type, and within the group by an item number.

Entries: Item number, title, source or publisher, color or b/w, length, number of frames or of pages or of items, cost, 15–25-word description of content.

Special Features: Index to numbered instructional media sources; bibliography.

31. **A Directory of Safety Films,** by the Accident Prevention Committee, American Academy of Pediatrics, 1801 Hinman Ave., Evanston, Ill. 60204. 1963. Free. Limited supply. 80p.

Scope: A directory of 150 child safety 16mm films dealing with babysitting, bicycles, scooters, farm, fire, home, first aid, guns, pedestrian, water safety, railroads, school safety, traffic and general safety. Inclusion does not necessarily indicate endorsement.

Arrangement: Alphabetical by title. Subject index.

Entries: Title, producer, date, screening time, sound or silent, color or b/w, interest level, availability information is to be obtained from local and state sources, descriptive annotation of 15–60 words.

Special Features: List of major film libraries in each state and a list of local and national film sources.

32. **Educational Media Index: A Project of the Educational Media Council.** McGraw-Hill Book Co., New York, N.Y. 10036. 1964. $62.45. 14v. Individual volumes available separately at various prices. (Limited supply available from Educational Media Council, Inc., Du Pont Circle Building, Suite 710, 1346 Connecticut Ave., N.W., Washington, D.C. 20036)

Scope: Approximately 28,000 titles of educational motion pictures, filmstrips, kinescopes, charts, graphs, maps in sets, cross-media kits, flat pictures in sets, models, mock-ups, phonodiscs, phonotapes, programed instructional materials, slides, transparencies, and videotapes available for educational use anywhere in the United States. The materials range in level of use from kindergarten through college and adult education and include the following subjects: agricultural education, art, business education, economics, engineering, English language, foreign language, geography, guidance, health, history, home economics, industrial education, mathematics, music, political science, psychology, safety, science, and teacher education.

Arrangement: Volumes 1 through 13 are arranged by subject, with volume 1 listing materials appropriate for kindergarten through grade 3 and volume 2 including materials appropriate for grades 4 through 6. Both volumes cover all subjects of the elementary school curriculum. Volumes 3 through 13 are subject indexes and include materials appropriate for grades 7 through college and adult education. The subjects in sequential order of volumes are: art and music, business education and training, English language, foreign language, guidance, psychology and teacher education, health-safety and home economics, industrial and agricultural education, mathematics, science and engineering, geography and history, and economics and political science. Volume 14 is a master title index and lists items found in volumes 1 through 13. Part 1 of each volume lists the subject headings and indexes their location by volume. Part 2, descriptive entries, is alphabetically arranged by subject, but in some volumes the subject arrangement is further subdivided into sections. Part 3 of each volume is a title index which lists the subject headings under which individual titles may be found.

Entries: Main subject heading, symbol denoting type of medium, title, producer or publisher, distributor, running time, number of frames or discs or items in sets, size (mm), speed (rpm, ips), color or b/w, series title, grade level, date of production, availability for television, purchase and rental price, study guide or related materials if any, descriptive annotation varying in length from 1 to 16 lines.

Special Features: Use of symbols before descriptive entries to denote type of medium and key to the 14 symbols which appears in lower left-hand corner of each even-numbered page; colored strip on front cover varying for each volume; master title index.

33. **Educational Sound Filmstrip Directory,** compiled and distributed by Du Kane Corporation, Audio Visual Division, St. Charles, Ill. 60174. 5th ed. 1969. Free. 20p. Also available May 1970 1-page addendum listing "Additional Educational Sound Filmstrip Sources."

Scope: More than 5,500 individual and series titles of sound filmstrips in the following subject areas: art, business and economics, language arts, mathematics, music, physical education and sports, science, social studies, teacher education, and vocational education. Listings are based upon information furnished by producers.

Arrangement: Classified by subject, and alphabetical by title under appropriate subject headings.

Entries: Title, producer code, number of filmstrips, color or b/w.

Special Features: Directory of producers.

34. Educators Guide to Free Films, compiled and edited by Mary Foley Horkheimer and John W. Diffor. 29th ed. Educators Progress Service, Randolph, Wis. 53956. 1970. $10.75. 790p. Revised annually.

Scope: Motion pictures in all instructional subjects, including accident prevention, agriculture, aviation, business education, geography, health, history, home economics, music, and science. Currently available free of charge on loan to school superintendents, teachers, audiovisual instructors, and librarians. 5,002 titles.

Arrangement: Alphabetical by title under subject areas, with title and detailed subject index.

Entries: Title, distributor, date, running time, silent or sound, color or b/w, availability, descriptive annotation in 10–70 words.

Special Features: Source and availability index gives terms of loan and length of time necessary for booking; television clearance; availability in Canada; various sections of the *Guide* distinguished by different-colored paper.

35. Educators Guide to Free Filmstrips, compiled and edited by Mary Foley Horkheimer and John W. Diffor. 21st ed. Educators Progress Service, Randolph, Wis. 53956. 1970. $8.50. 184p. Revised annually. Earlier editions have title *Educators Guide to Free Slidefilms.*

Scope: Filmstrips and slides in all instructional subjects currently available free of charge, either on loan or as gift. 462 titles, including 303 filmstrips, 157 sets of slides, and 2 sets of transparencies.

Arrangement: Alphabetical by title under subject areas, with title index and detailed subject index.

Entries: Title, distributor, date, running time or number of frames or slides, availability of script or phonodiscs, silent or sound, color or b/w, descriptive annotation in 10–70 words.

Special Features: Introduction gives suggestions on how to use filmstrips and how to obtain them; source and availability index gives terms of loan and length of time necessary for booking for each distributor; various sections of the *Guide* distinguished by use of different-colored paper.

36. Educators Guide to Free Guidance Materials, compiled and edited by Mary H. Saterstrom and Joe E. Steph, with Gail F. Farwell. 8th ed. Educators Progress Service, Randolph, Wis. 53956. 1970. $8.75. 254p. Revised annually.

Scope: Generally available free and free-loan educational and informational guidance films, filmstrips, tapes, phonorecords, and other supplementary materials, such as bulletins, pamphlets, study guides, handbooks, charts, posters, brochures, and books. 982 items, including 571 films, 64 filmstrips, 59 tapes and transcriptions, and 288 other supplementary materials on guidance.

Arrangement: Classified by medium and by guidance categories or areas, then alphabetical by title. Title and detailed subject indexes.

Entries: Title, distributor or producer or publisher, author, date, running time or number of frames or number of pages, speed, silent or sound, full color, availability of scripts or phonodiscs to accompany filmstrips, limitations of distribution, descriptive annotation of 20–50 words.

Special Features: Film sources, their addresses, terms of loans, time necessary for bookings, television clearance, availability in Canada and ability of distributor to fill requests; various sections of the *Guide* distinguished by use of different-colored paper; general directions for obtaining the material given in the Introduction.

37. **Educators Guide to Free Health, Physical Education and Recreation Materials,** compiled and edited by Foley A. Horkheimer. 3d ed. Educators Progress Service, Randolph, Wis. 53956. 1970. $8. 456p. Revised annually.

Scope: Selected, currently available free and free-loan films, filmstrips, phonotapes, transcriptions, and other materials such as bulletins, pamphlets, charts, exhibits, posters, maps, magazines, and books. 2,197 items including 1,266 films, 129 filmstrips, 48 phonotapes, 45 transcriptions, and 705 other types of materials. Subjects include: accident prevention, diseases, first aid, foods and nutrition, personal health and hygiene, public health, safety, sanitation, sex education, sports.

Arrangement: Classified by medium and subject, then alphabetical by title. Title and detailed subject index.

Entries: Title, date, running time or number of frames or pages, speed, silent or sound, color or b/w, interest level, availability of scripts or phonodiscs to accompany filmstrips, limitations of distribution, descriptive annotation of 20–50 words, producer or distributor or publisher, author.

Special Features: Source and availability index, terms of loans, time necessary for bookings, television clearance, availability in Canada, and ability of distributor to fill requests; various sections of the *Guide* distinguished by use of different-colored paper; general directions for obtaining the material given in the Introduction.

38. **Educators Guide to Free Science Materials,** compiled and edited by Mary Horkheimer Saterstrom and John W. Renner. 10th ed. Educators Progress Service, Randolph, Wis. 53956. 1970. $9.25. 451p. Revised annually.

Scope: Generally available free and free-loan educational and informational science films, filmstrips, and other supplementary materials such as bulletins, pamphlets, exhibits, charts, posters, and books. 1,937 items, including 1,258 films, 114 filmstrips, 69 tapes and transcriptions, and 496 other supplementary materials on science.

Arrangement: Classified by medium and subject, then alphabetical by title. Title and detailed subject indexes.

Entries: Title, distributor or producer or publisher, author, date, running time, number of frames or pages, availability of scripts or phonodiscs to accompany filmstrips, limitations of distribution, descriptive annotation of 20–50 words.

Special Features: Film sources, their addresses, terms of loans, time necessary for bookings, and ability of distributor to fill requests; 8 sample curriculum units demonstrate the use of materials listed in the *Guide;* various sections of the *Guide* distinguished by use of different-colored paper; general directions for obtaining the material given in the Introduction.

39. Educators Guide to Free Social Studies Materials, compiled and edited by Patricia H. Suttles with William H. Hartley. 9th ed. Educators Progress Service, Randolph, Wis. 53956. 1970. $9.50. 563p. Revised annually.

Scope: Generally available free and free-loan educational and informational social studies films, filmstrips, sets of slides, tapes, scripts, phonorecords, and other supplementary materials such as bulletins, pamphlets, exhibits, charts, posters, and books. 2,663 items, including 1,758 films, 78 flimstrips, 83 sets of slides, 210 tapes, 17 scripts, 56 transcripts, and 461 printed materials on social studies.

Arrangement: Classified by medium and subject, then alphabetical by title. Title and detailed subject indexes.

Entries: Title, distributor or producer or publisher, author, date, running time or number of frames or pages, speed, silent or sound, full color, interest level, availability of scripts of phonodiscs to accompany filmstrips, limitations of distribution, descriptive annotation of 20–50 words.

Special Features: Film sources, their addresses, terms of loans, time necessary for bookings, television clearance, availability in Canada, and ability of distributor to fill requests; various sections of the *Guide* distinguished by use of different-colored paper; general directions for obtaining the material given in the Introduction.

40. Educators Guide to Free Tapes, Scripts, and Transcriptions, compiled and edited by Walter A. Wittich. 16th ed. Educators Progress

Service, Randolph, Wis. 53956. 1970. $7.75. 200p. Revised annually.

Scope: Audio materials in the form of phonotapes, scripts, and phonodiscs in all instructional subjects, including conservation, guidance, health education, homemaking, language arts, music, science, and social studies. Available on free loan to school superintendents, audiovisual education directors, librarians, and teachers. 375 titles, including 298 tapes, 15 scripts, and 62 transcriptions.

Arrangement: Alphabetical by title under subject areas, with title and subject indexes.

Entries: Title, distributor, date, running time, speed (rpm or ips) of transcriptions, availability, descriptive annotation in 100–50 words summarizing the story.

Special Features: Source and availability index gives terms of loan, address, and length of time necessary for booking for each distributor; various sections of the *Guide* distinguished by different-colored paper.

41. **EFLA Evaluations.** Educational Film Library Association, Inc., 17 W. Sixtieth St., New York, N.Y. 10023. 1948 to date. *Film Evaluation Guide,* 1946–64, cumulates approximately 5,000 EFLA Evaluations, and *1968 Supplement* includes an additional 2,252 evaluations (for details see separate entry). 1964–66 *Evaluation Card Supplement* of 700 recent evaluations on 3″ x 5″ cards. $15. Available to members only. Membership $25 per year plus service-basis charge depending on size of film library. Monthly listings on 3″ x 5″ cards sent to members as issued, 36 cards per month.

Scope: Motion pictures in all instructional subjects currently produced. Approximately 7,250 motion pictures had been evaluated by 1968 at the rate of 36–40 per month.

Arrangement: Single card per motion-picture title. Duplicate cards may be purchased to form subject file.

Entries: Title, distributor, producer, date, running time, silent or sound, color or b/w, cost for purchase or loan, interest level, name of evaluating institution, Dewey Decimal Classification number and Library of Congress card number when available, general rating, descriptive annotation giving synopsis in 30–50 words, technical rating, and evaluative annotation giving uses, appeal, and importance of film in 40–50 words.

Special Features: Subject headings suggested; EFLA card number given.

Authors' Note: A guide to the 3,900 motion pictures reviewed on cards by the Educational Film Library Association from 1948 through August 31, 1959, is the *Index to EFLA Evaluations,* compiled by Elizabeth Flory and edited by Emily S. Jones, Educational Film Library Association, Inc., 17 W. Sixtieth St., New York, N.Y. 10023. 67p. Free to members.

42. 8mm Film Directory, compiled and edited by Grace Ann Kone. Published by the Educational Film Library Association, Inc. Available from Comprehensive Service Corporation, 250 W. Sixty-fourth St., New York, N.Y. 10023. 1969. $10.50. 532p.

Scope: Intended to include all 8mm films, regardless of length or subject matter, in distribution in the United States. The list is comprehensive with no attempt to screen or select qualitatively. Omissions are attributed to failure of distributor/producer to send necessary information. Includes all 8mm film formats—standard or super, silent or sound, cartridge or reel-to-reel. Subject areas include: arts, education, fiction, language, recreation, religion, sciences, society and environment, and technology.

Arrangement: Alphabetical by title under appropriate subdivisions of 9 major subject areas.

Entries: Title, series title, production date (if available), Dewey Decimal Classification number, running time, grade level (if available), sound or silent, cartridge, loop, or reel-to-reel, standard or super, and length in minutes or feet, producer or distributor, 10–40 word description of content.

Special Features: Introduction explaining 8mm formats and developments in the field by Emily Jones; how to use the directory; producer and distributor index; 8mm motion-picture equipment specifications and photographs; key to Dewey Decimal Classification; alphabetical index of films and subjects.

43. 8mm Films in Medicine and Health Sciences, compiled by Reba A. Benschoter. Communications Division, University of Nebraska, College of Medicine, 602 S. Forty-fourth Ave., Omaha, Neb. 68105. Survey supported by Public Health Service and National Library of Medicine. 1969. $3.50. 318p.

Scope: More than 1,000 entries of 8mm medical and health science films produced both commercially and privately.

Arrangement: Alphabetical by title under 22 subject headings—anatomy, basic sciences, cancer, clinical medicine, dermatology, embryology, first aid and safety, health services and education, hospital food service, hospital housekeeping, hospital ward clerk training, nursing, obstetrics, ophthalmology, patient education (adult), patient education (child), pharmacology, psychiatry and psychology, radiology, rehabilitation, surgery, and technology (medical).

Entries: Title, producer, production date if available, production credits, length, sound or silent, color or b/w, type of 8mm format, educational author credits, 20–40-word content summary, distributor, price.

Special Features: Survey report summary; selected bibliography; title index; distributors' address listing; loose-leaf format.

44. The Elementary School Library Collection: A Guide to Books and Other Media. Phases 1-2-3. 5th ed. Mary V. Gaver, general editor. The Bro-Dart Foundation, 113 Frelinghuysen Ave., Newark, N.J. 07114. 1970. $20 including the *Supplement.* 710p. *Supplement* 1970. 193p. (6th ed. 1971, in progress)

Scope: An annotated classified (Dewey Abridged edition) catalog of more than 7,800 titles, including approximately 2,000 audio-visual items and more than 60 periodicals considered basic for any school library serving grades kindergarten through 6; *Supplement* includes approximately 2,200 titles of which approximately 700 are audiovisual items and an additional 13 are periodicals. The catalog is divided into 6 groups of materials: reference, nonfiction, fiction, easy, periodicals, and professional tools. Audiovisual media include charts, kits, 8mm loops, transparencies, filmstrips, phonodiscs, slides, and study and art prints. They are integrated with the books but are also listed separately by classification number in a section at the end of the book. The collection is divided into 3 phases related to school size. Phase 1 presents the minimum-sized effective collection for the small school. Phases 2 and 3 progressively increase the total number of titles, including professional and audiovisual materials. The catalog is a continuing program with entries evaluated and reevaluated by a selection committee and its chairman, who is the general editor. The publication has gone through 5 editions in 5 years and is one of the largest existing examples of a complex list which has been computer-produced, computer-arranged, and computer-composed.

Arrangement: Main body is arranged by Dewey Decimal Classification number; other sections are: author index, title index, subject index, a graded list of materials for nursery through 2.2 levels, a classified list of audiovisual media, and a list of the large-print books included in the catalog.

Entries: Dewey decimal number and symbol denoting type of medium (if nonprint); author or composer; title; edition; publisher or producer; distributor; date; series note; teacher's guide (if available) grade level; price; illustrations; color or b/w; sound; number of pages, frames, sides, discs, or items in sets; diameter in inches; speed (rpm or ips); type of format for 8mm titles; subject headings; and descriptive annotation. Beginning with the *Supplement,* the Edward B. Fry interest-reading level is designated for many books.

Special Features: Statement of selection policy including an analysis of curricular developments emerging in recent practice; directory of publishers; classification principles and policies; outline of the Dewey Decimal Classification system; separate author and title indexes; classified listing of audiovisual materials and large-print books; sections of the book distinguished by the use of colored divider pages. ". . . an ambitious effort to provide a closer estimate of the appeal and difficulty of reading material for children . . . a double symbol, the first half of which is a letter indicating our estimate of reader interest or appeal, the second half of which is a *number* indicating our estimate of reading difficulty (e.g. P/2, I/4, P/6, A/8)" (Preface).

45. **The Encyclopaedia Cinematographica—English Translation of Film Titles Listed in 1967 Index,** edited by G. Wolf, Institut fur den Wissenchaftlichen Film, Gottingen, West Germany. Available from Director of the American Archive of Encyclopaedia Cinematographica, Leslie P. Greenhill, 203C Old Main, Pennsylvania State University, University Park, Pa. 16802. 1967. Free. 56p. *Supplement.* 1969. Free. 16p. (New edition scheduled for publication)

Scope: Approximately 1,500 scientific films (mostly silent) are indexed in the main volume and its supplement. Films have been submitted by scientists throughout the world and considered by an international board with headquarters in Germany to have a high degree of authenticity and scientific accuracy and to depict a single phenomenon which cannot be observed by the unaided human, which needs to be compared with other phenomena, or which does not occur frequently. Subjects include: zoology, physiology, invertebrata, vertebrata, amphibia, aves, mammalia, cytology, microbiology, oceania, botany, technology (sciences techniques).

Arrangement: Alphabetical by title within broad subject areas.

Entries: Title (original language, English translation), date, color or b/w, sound if applicable, length, scientist, country of origin.

Special Features: Procedures for submitting scientific films.

46. **Entelek CAI/CMI/PI Information Exchange.** Entelek Inc., 42 Pleasant St., Newburyport, Mass. 01950. 1965 to date. Membership $150 per year. Monthly listings on 5" x 8" cards bound in book form (cards are perforated for removing and filing or may be shelved as a book), 14–20 programs per issue.

Scope: Currently released computer-assisted (CAI), computer-managed (CMI), and programed instruction (PI) programs in all subject fields and grade levels. Also includes index cards for currently released CAI, CMI, and PI research reports and descriptions of CAI facilities.

Arrangement: Numerical according to Entelek serial number.

Entries: Dewey Decimal Classification number, author number, Entelek serial number, title, subject field, author(s), target audience, curriculum relationships, program length, instructional logic, instructional language, computer, input-output devices, auxiliary materials, evaluation results, availability of related programs, source, sponsor.

Special Features: 5 copies of the 5" x 8" basic information card for each program are included to provide a serial number file, a Dewey number file, an institution file, an author file, a call number file, or such special files as computer-language or computer-model file. Cards for each type of index are color cued. Subscribers also receive a monthly newsletter, working papers and reprints on CAI and CMI topics at irregular intervals, microfiche copies of all research abstracts, program specifications, and facility descriptions distributed prior to the date of subscription. Subscribers also receive printed dividers to facilitate cross-indexing cards.

47. **Ethnic Studies and Audiovisual Media: A Listing and Discussion,** by Harold A. Layer, San Francisco State College. An Occasional Paper from the ERIC Clearinghouse on Educational Media and Technology at the Institute for Communication Research, Stanford University, Stanford, Calif. 94305. 1969. Single copies free. 11p.

Scope: Approximately 270 films, filmstrips, audiotapes, records, videotapes, and transparencies. Subject areas include: general ethnic studies, Asian-American studies, black studies, Mexican Spanish-American studies, and native American studies.

Arrangement: Alphabetical by title under subject area.

Entries: Title, medium, distributor, availability, 5–10-word description.

Special Features: Introductory pages discussing ethnic studies and audiovisual materials; distributor index.

48. **Fact Book.** National Instructional Television Center [Box A, Bloomington, Ind. 47401] 1971. Single copies free upon request. 28p.

Scope: Approximately 100 series of telecourses designed for specific instructional goals and grade levels and available from the National Instructional Television Center. Subject areas include: art, communications, early childhood, economics, foreign language, guidance, health and physical education, humanities, language arts, mathematics, science, social studies, computer technology, engineering, physics, psychology, and sociology.

Arrangement: Divided into 3 sections. Section 1 is divided according to subject areas, which are alphabetically arranged and under which are listed descriptions of telecourses alphabetically by title. Section 2 is arranged by grade level, under which telecourses are listed alphabetically by title. Section 3 is a subject area listing with subjects listed alphabetically under which telecourses are alphabetically listed.

Entries: Section 1—title, 25–100-word descriptive annotation. Sections 2 and 3—title, number of lessons, and length per lesson. *Special Features:* Foreword providing background information on the Center and some of the telecourses; procedures for users; information services; National Advisory Board and Administrative Staff.

49. **Feature Films on 8 and 16: A Directory of 8mm and 16mm Sound Feature Films Available for Rental in the United States,** edited by James L. Limbacher. 3d ed. Educational Film Library Association, Inc., 17 W. Sixtieth St., New York, N.Y. 10023. 1970. $8. 350p.
Scope: More than 3,000 entries compiled from the best-known rental libraries from all areas of the United States. Contains an estimated 90 percent of all feature films generally available in 8mm and 16mm in the United States. Documentaries, animated cartoons, and films with no professional casts are also included.
Arrangement: Alphabetical by title.
Entries: Title, date, names of stars, running time, distributor, type (feature, documentary, or animated cartoon), color or b/w, country, technical information.
Special Features: Names, addresses, and telephone numbers of distributors; director index.

50. **Film Evaluation Guide, 1946–64.** Educational Film Library Association, Inc., 17 W. Sixtieth St., New York, N.Y. 10023. 1965. $30; $25 to EFLA members. 528p. *Supplement.* 1968. $12; $10 to EFLA members. 157p. (1967–70 *Supplement* being published)
Scope: Approximately 7,250 16mm films evaluated and annotated by EFLA volunteer preview committees. Represents a selected compilation of annotations originally released as 3″ x 5″ film evaluation cards distributed by EFLA to members from 1948–67. Includes films on more than 500 subjects. Annotations provide basic bibliographic and content information and evaluations. All titles were checked to make sure that they were still available and that the price, distributor, and addresses were correct. The *Guide* is not a complete directory of all available films, nor is it a selected list of recommended films. Annotations appear as they were originally submitted, generally a few months after the date of production. They have not been rewritten in view of changes in events, points of view, or standards of film production.
Arrangement: Alphabetical by title. Subject list of titles, arranged by the Dewey Decimal Classification system. Subject key to Dewey Decimal Classification system.
Entries: Title, producer, distributor, address of distributor, production date, purchase price, running time, silent or sound, b/w or color, subject area, name(s) of evaluator(s), synopsis of 20–60 words, suggested uses, age level, rating of technical qual-

ities, a critical overall evaluation in 40–50 words, Dewey Decimal Classification number, and EFLA card number.

Special Features: History of the EFLA Evaluation Program; information concerning EFLA activities, publications, and types of membership.

51. **Film Guide for Marketing Executives,** edited by William Wachs, Rutgers University. Sales and Marketing Executives—International, 630 Third Ave., New York, N.Y. 10017. 1966. $4.95. 71p.

Scope: Approximately 300 motion pictures and filmstrips. Subject categories include: advertising, merchandising and sales promotion, consumer product and retailing, public and customer relations, sales management, sales meetings and miscellaneous, and sales training and selling techniques. Inclusion does not mean endorsement.

Arrangement: Alphabetical by subject categories. Subject categories are subdivided into motion pictures and filmstrips. Titles are alphabetical under type of medium.

Entries: Title, running time, color or b/w, loan or rental, source, 10–100-word descriptive annotation.

Special Features: Introductory sections describe the conduct of meetings using films, suggestions for getting a film produced, and a checklist of applications; source index; bibliography.

52. **Film Guide for Music Educators,** by Donald J. Shelter. 2d ed. Music Educators National Conference, National Education Association, 1201 Sixteenth St., N.W., Washington, D.C. 20036. 1968. $2.50. 90p.

Scope: Approximately 560 films and 50 filmstrips designed for teaching music, especially at the secondary level. Some titles were originally produced for use on instructional or educational television, others for commercial television and still others for a specific area and level of teaching. Comparative ratings have been eliminated. General categories are: musical performance, history of music (and biographies), band, orchestra, teaching of music, visual interpretation of music, acoustics, music as a career, and music festivals.

Arrangement: Alphabetical by title under medium.

Entries: Title, distributor, date, running time, color or b/w, 20–50-word descriptive annotation, suggested audiences.

Special Features: Title index; subject index; bibliography; producer and distributor index.

53. **Film Guide on Chemicals, Chemistry and the Chemical Industry.** 1969–70 ed. Manufacturing Chemists' Association Inc., 1825 Connecticut Ave., N.W., Washington, D.C. 20009. 1967. Free. 24p.

Scope: 16mm films and a few filmstrips covering many facets of chemicals, chemistry, and the chemical industry suitable for audiences ranging from teachers and students to business, civic, and social groups. A few of the subject headings include: chemistry and agriculture; chemistry experiments; and chemistry for/in petroleum, construction, better health, home economics, research, pesticides, safety, plastics, and vocational guidance. More than 300 film entries.

Arrangement: Classified by subject. Title and subject indexes.

Entries: Title, running time, color or b/w, sound or silent, source or contact (since most titles are sponsored, they are loaned free), interest level, television clearance, a descriptive annotation of 30–60 words.

Special Features: Directory of sources.

54. **Film Reference Guide for Medicine and Allied Sciences.** U.S. Department of Health, Education and Welfare, National Library of Medicine, National Medical Audiovisual Center, Atlanta, Ga. 30333. Available from the Superintendent of Documents, U.S. Government Printing Office, Washington, D.C. 20402. 1968. $2.75. 386p. *Supplement* published 1969. 75c. 74p. (Each annual issue supersedes preceding issues; new edition scheduled.)

Scope: Includes selected medical motion pictures and filmstrips currently being used in the medical program of at least one of the member agencies of the Federal Advisory Council on Medical Training Aids and currently available for loan or rental. No films are listed which are for sale only. Major subject areas covered are: accidents and accident prevention, alcohol or drug addiction, biology, cancer, cardio-vascular system, chemistry, child care and maternal welfare, civil defense, dentistry, digestive system, ear, environmental health, eye, first aid, microbiology, neurology, nutrition, pharmacology, psychiatry, surgery, veterinary medicine, and zoology. Approximately 3,000 entries.

Arrangement: Alphabetical by title under subjects. Title index. List of subjects and subheads used.

Entries: Title, producer/sponsor, country of origin, date, releasing agent, series title if any, running time or number of frames if a filmstrip, color or b/w, sound or silent, type of medium, size (mm), distributors, credits, availability information; 30–150-word descriptive annotation.

Special Features: Directory of distributors.

55. **A Filmography of Films about Movies and Movie Making,** by Robert W. Wagner and David L. Parker. Eastman Kodak Co., Department 454, Rochester, N.Y. 14650. 1969. 10 for $1; 100 for $10. 11p.

Scope: Contains the titles of some 169 films on the subject of movie-making. Includes films on the mechanics of splicing, basic animation techniques, directing, composition, planning, lighting, editing, set construction, facts about film, the history of cinema, and the future of the film medium. All titles listed are 16mm, b/w, sound films unless otherwise noted.

Arrangement: Alphabetical by title.

Entries: Title, producer and/or distributor, running time, color, brief description of content in 10–50 words.

Special Features: An alphabetical listing of sources of films about movies and move-making, with addresses.

56. **Films and Filmstrips for Art Education K–12.** Curriculum Development Center, New York State Education Department. The University of the State of New York, Albany, N.Y. 12224. 1965. 25c. 34p. Single copies only may be purchased; remittance must accompany order.

Scope: Selected films and filmstrips to supplement art education program throughout school year, rather than to be used in a short, concentrated period of time. More than 220 motion pictures and more than 60 filmstrips which became available before June 1962; those produced before 1945 are not included unless they are of outstanding value. Subjects include: art appreciation, drawing and painting, graphics, sculpture, ceramics, design, and general crafts.

Arrangement: Alphabetical by title under type of medium.

Entries: Title or series title, running time, distributor/producer, a 20–80-word descriptive annotation.

Special Features: Sources for 2″ x 2″ slides; a survey chart of films and filmstrips alphabetically listed, giving title, page on which annotation appears, level, distributor, and subject areas.

57. **Films and Filmstrips for the Space Age.** Rev. ed. Educational Film Library Association, Inc., 17 W. Sixtieth St., New York, N.Y. 10023. 1967. $1. 8p. (EFLA Service Supplement) (Revision scheduled for 1971)

Scope: More than 120 entries of motion pictures and filmstrips on the space age, covering such subject areas as: history and future of space travel, research and principles of the space age, guided missiles, and unmanned satellites.

Arrangement: Alphabetical by title under subject.

Entries: Title, producer/distributor, date, running time, sound or silent, color or b/w, number of frames if a filmstrip, a brief statement of content.

Special Features: Directory of sources.

58. **Films and Filmstrips on Audio-Visual Materials and Methods.** Educational Film Library Association, Inc., 17 W. Sixtieth St., New York, N.Y. 10023. 1960. $1. 14p. (EFLA Service Supplement) (Revision scheduled for 1971)

Scope: Motion pictures and filmstrips covering many phases of the audiovisual field, including field trips, motion-picture history and development, animation, still photography, research and theory, and utilization. An inclusive list—except in areas which have much material—intended for teachers, audiovisual coordinators or directors, and students in AV education courses.

Arrangement: Classified by subject, then alphabetical by title.

Entries: Title, producer and distributor, date, running time or number of frames, sound or silent, color or b/w, descriptive annotations of 10–40 words.

Special Features: Directory of sources.

59. Films and Filmstrips on Forestry, edited by Nelson T. Samson. Rev. ed. School of Forestry, Stephen F. Austin State College, Nacogdoches, Tex. 75961. 1969. Apply. 93p. (Bulletin 17, April 1969, revision of Bulletin 7, *Films and Filmstrips on Forestry,* April 1965)

Scope: Films and filmstrips on forestry and related subjects, including utilization of lumber, paper, and plywood, seasoning and preservation, logging and sawmilling, safety, forest fires, insects and disease, trees, conservation, and mapping and photogrammetry. 548 films and 74 filmstrips.

Arrangement: Films, alphabetical by title. Filmstrips, in a separate section, alphabetical by title. Subject index.

Entries: Title, running time or number of frames, color or b/w, sound or silent, source, a few release dates, geographic limitations on distribution if any, 15–75-word descriptive annotation.

Special Features: List of 168 sources.

60. Films and Librarians: A Selected List of 16mm Films Useful in the Field of Librarianship, compiled by Beatrice S. Simmons. (Reprinted from *Illinois Libraries*) New Mexico Research Library of the Southwest, P.O. Box 4725, Santa Fe, N. Mex. 87501. 1970. $1.25. 12p.

Scope: 48 films recommended for their usefulness in the field of librarianship.

Arrangement: Alphabetical by title.

Entries: Title, length, color or b/w, production date, producer/distributor with address, 50–200-word description of content, recommended teaching purpose or use.

61. Films for Children. Educational Film Library Association, Inc., 17 W. Sixtieth St., New York, N.Y. 10023. 1961. 59p. *Supplement.* 1965. $2. 14p. Available only in combined edition. (Revision scheduled for 1971)

Scope: Selected list of 272 16mm films (including the Supplement). Categories are: animation, circus, farm and zoo, fables, legends, fairy tales, holidays, nature and wildlife, pets, puppets, real life adventure, story films, and silent film comedies. "Films for Children," as interpreted by the contributors, means not classroom or informational films, but those which children watch for the same reasons that they read good children's books—for entertainment.

Arrangement: Alphabetical by title under category or subject.

Entries: Title, producer/distributors, running time, color or b/w, date (not included in the Supplement), a descriptive annotation of 20–60 words.

Special Features: Directory of distributors; articles on how to select and use films in programs for children.

62. **Films for Children: A Selected List,** prepared by the New York Library Association, Children's and Young Adult Services Section. Rev. ed. Available from New York Library Association, P.O. Box 521, Woodside, N.Y. 11377. 1969. $1. 32p.

Scope: Approximately 100 carefully chosen 16mm motion pictures for children, representing a wide range of subjects. Classroom films are not included unless they were considered to be of outstanding quality (e.g., Walt Disney's *Secrets of the Bee World*). Included in the Introduction are the criteria for selection, useful hints on film programing, and a bibliography of articles about film programs.

Arrangement: Alphabetical by title with subject index.

Entries: Title, producer/distributor, date, running time, b/w or color, sales price, lengthy descriptive annotation.

Special Features: Suggestions for film programing; bibliography; distributors with addresses.

63. **Films for Early Childhood Education,** compiled by ACEI Nursery School Education Committee. Association for Childhood Education International, 3615 Wisconsin Ave., N.W., Washington, D.C. 20016. 1968. 50c; 5 for $2. 17p.

Scope: Approximately 60 films of educational value to young children. Prepared by the ACEI Nursery School Education Committee from suggestions by state ACE vice-presidents representing nursery schools; Head Start regional training officers; members of the Direction Seminar, Information Retrieval Center for the Disadvantaged; and the ERIC Clearinghouse on Early Childhood Education. Subject areas include: early childhood program; special early childhood curriculum interests; child development; problems of young children; parent-teacher relationships.

Arrangement: Alphabetical by subject and then alphabetical by title.

Entries: Title, producer, distributor, running time, color or b/w, 30–50-word descriptive annotation, call number of film if available, suggested audience.

Special Features: Selected list of ACEI publications.

64. **Films for Libraries,** selected by a subcommittee of the Audio-Visual

Committee, American Library Association, 50 East Huron St., Chicago, Ill. 60611. 1962. $1.75. 81p.

Scope: A selected, annotated list of more than 400 16mm motion pictures considered by the subcommittee in consultation with film librarians across the country to be the best films currently available for library collections. Highly technical films and those which are primarily curriculum oriented are not included. Classics in the documentary field, experimental and avant-garde films, and a few film series of outstanding interest are included. Children's librarians will find here traditional fairy tales and fantasies, and unusual films on animals, hobbies, and other subjects of interest to children. Teachers from elementary grades through college can use many of the films as a means of supplementing the curriculum. Youth workers and community leaders will find titles to stimulate discussion of many subjects and issues.

Arrangement: Alphabetical by title. Subject index.

Entries: Title, producer/distributor, date, running time, color or b/w, price, interest level, descriptive annotation of 30–100 words.

Special Features: Directory of distributors.

65. **Films for Music Education and Opera Films: An International Selective Catalogue,** compiled by the International Music Centre, Vienna, and published by UNESCO. Available from UNESCO Publications Center, P.O. Box 433, New York, N.Y. 10016. 1962. $1.25. 114p.

Scope: 117 titles from 17 countries on music education and 39 titles from 9 countries on opera films. Subject areas under music education include: history of music and composers, instruments, orchestras and bands, musicians perform, study and teaching, music camps and study centers, and experimental and jazz.

Arrangement: Divided into two parts—part 1, films for music education, and part 2, opera films. Each section is preceded by an introduction and by a title index giving entry number. Titles are arranged according to entry number.

Entries: Title, country, producer, distributor, running time, date, color or b/w, type of medium, language, 20–50-word descriptive annotation.

Special Features: Title index; index by countries; index by composers.

66. **Films for Personnel Management: An Annotated Directory of 16mm Films, Filmstrips, and Videotapes,** by Louis S. Goodman and Associates. Educational Film Library Association, Inc., 17 W. Sixtieth St., New York, N.Y. 10023. 1969. $5. 116p.

Scope: Approximately 300 entries selected for use by personnel directors and managers, training directors, and specialists in labor and industrial relations, management development, and employee relations. Entries are concerned with apprenticeship, attitudes and morale, collective bargaining, communication, community relations, conferences and meetings, discipline, economics, grievances arbitration, human relations, insurance, job evaluation, leadership and supervision, management skills, motivation, performance appraisal, recruiting and interviewing, safety, social security, retirement, suggestions, and training.

Arrangement: Main section, alphabetical by subject and within subjects, alphabetical by title; alphabetical title index includes series titles but not individual titles which are parts of series.

Entries: Title, running time and/or number of frames, color or b/w, date, producer, descriptive annotation of 20–50 words, purchase and rental source.

Special Features: Source index; introduction entitled "How to Use This Book."

67. **Films for Young Adults: A Selected List,** prepared by New York Library Association, Children's and Young Adult Services Section. Rev. ed. Published by and available from Educational Film Library Association, Inc., 17 W. Sixtieth St., New York, N.Y. 10023. 1970. $2. 54p.

Scope: A selected list of approximately 125 representative 16mm motion pictures of interest to young people of approximately 13–18 years of age. Although classroom films as such are not included unless of exceptional quality, films in the fields of art, language arts, science, and social studies will have many uses in formal education. The introduction to the list provides the criteria for selection and offers hints on programing, publicity, and setting up equipment; short bibliography of related readings and recommended periodicals. The long, descriptive annotations suggest books and other films that can be used with these selections for a complete program.

Arrangement: Alphabetical by title with a subject index.

Entries: Title, producer/distributor, date, running time, b/w or color, sales price, lengthy descriptive annotation.

Special Features: Bibliography of articles about films and film programs; recommended periodicals; alphabetical list of film makers; list of distributors with addresses.

68. **Films in the Behavioral Sciences: An Annotated Catalogue.** John M. Schneider, Barnett Addis, and Marsha Addis. 2d ed. Behavioral Sciences Media Laboratory, Department of Psychiatry and Behavioral Sciences, University of Oklahoma Medical Center, Oklahoma City, Okla. 73104. August 1970. $4. 225p. Periodically revised or supplemented. Make checks or purchase orders payable to Behavioral Sciences Media Laboratory.

Scope: Approximately 1,300 16mm films reflecting the authors' expanded conceptualization of the type of films relevant to the teaching of the behavioral sciences. The second edition has numerous new film entries that relate to contemporary social issues as well as films that deal with basic research areas. Categories included are: phenomenology of behavior, personality influences on behavior, anthropological factors in behavior, sociological factors in behavior, hereditary factors in behavior, developmental bases of behavior, physiological factors in behavior, psychopathology, psychodynamics, therapeutic intervention, experimental psychopathology, historical perspectives and institutional treatment practices, psychopharmacology, brain and behavioral relations, learning, motivational and perceptual factors in behavior, sexual behavior, animal behavior and comparative psychological studies, role of the behavioral sciences in the practice of medicine, methods of evaluation and quantifying behavior. Titles are listed under several different categories where appropriate.

Arrangement: Alphabetical by category. Alphabetical by title.

Entries: Title, producer, distributors, date of release of film, running time, sound or silent, color or b/w, 30–100-word descriptive annotation, reference sources.

Special Features: Each film that was added after 1967 is designated with an asterisk; distributor listing.

69. **Films on Art,** compiled by Alfred W. Humphreys. No. 1 in a series of Publications sponsored by the Uses of Newer Media Project of the National Art Education Association, 1201 Sixteenth St., N.W., Washington, D.C. 20036. 1965. $1.50. 60p.

Scope: A listing of 2,050 8mm and 16mm films on art. Some of the items listed are not directly concerned with representing the visual arts but are included because they are in themselves examples of the artistic use of media. Subjects include: abstract art, architecture, artists, arts and crafts, calligraphy, ceramics, design, drafting, drawing, handicrafts, industrial art, interior decoration, jewelry, lithography, metal sculpture, mosaics, murals, museums, printing, puppets, sculpture, weaving, and woodworking.

Arrangement: Alphabetical by title.

Entries: Title, producer or distributor, date, running time, grade level, sound or silent, mm, color or b/w, price, and a descriptive word or phrase.

Special Features: List of producers and distributors.

70. **Films on Community Affairs: Urban and Rural,** compiled by Carolyn H. Kitterman, Indiana Department of Commerce. Available from

Council of Planning Librarians, P.O. Box 229, Monticello, Ill. 61856. August 1969. $6. 60p.

Scope: 251 films and filmstrips on urban and rural affairs. Areas included are: city planning, environmental control, housing, welfare, minority and intergroup relations, social organization and problems, health, rural areas development, and education. Inclusion or omission does not indicate recommendation. Attempt was made not to duplicate films in *Motion Picture Films on Planning, Housing, and Related Subjects—A Bibliography, Films for Action,* and *Films, Filmstrips, Slides, and Audio-Tapes on Housing and Community Development.*

Arrangement: Alphabetical by title.

Entries: Title, distributor, date if available, running time, color or b/w, rental price, call number of film if available, 20–80-word descriptive annotation.

Special Features: Title index; subject-headings index; subject index; distributor index.

71. **Films on Jobs, Training and the Ghetto: An Evaluative Guide.** American Foundation on Automation and Employment, Inc., 49 E. Sixty-eighth St., New York, N.Y. 10021. 1969. $5. 47p.

Scope: Includes approximately 211 titles of sound, 16mm films submitted by producers and distributors and screened and evaluated by panels designed to represent a variety of viewpoints of the major users of such films. Suggested as "an invaluable training aid for: top executives, personnel and training directors, training organizations and consultants, unions, government agencies, libraries and film libraries, schools and universities, and the mass media" (Preface).

Arrangement: Alphabetical by title.

Entries: Title, date, running time, color or b/w, producer, distributor, rental or purchase information, 20–25-word descriptive annotation, and an evaluation which is a summary of the views of the panels.

Special Features: Example of the evaluation form and explanation of its use; producers and distributors, with addresses.

72. **Films on Legal Subjects for Bar and Public Showings: A Listing of the Films and Sources,** compiled by the American Bar Association, Committee on Public Relations, 1155 E. Sixtieth St., Chicago, Ill. 60637. [1969.] Apply. 69p.

Scope: Motion pictures on legal and law-related subjects compiled to assist bar associations in obtaining films for showing to the public or at meetings of the bar, and to assist nonlawyer groups to find information about available legal films. Divided into 16 law-related subject areas, such as biographies, citizenship, communism, constitution, government, historical events, individual rights, international affairs, juvenile delinquency, the legal profession, medicine and law, and traffic laws and courts. Inclusion of films does not necessarily indicate endorsement of quality or content by the American Bar Association. More than 470 films.

Arrangement: Alphabetical by title under law-related subject headings and subheadings. Table of contents lists film titles alphabetically within categories.

Entries: Title, series title if in a series, running time, color or b/w, rental cost, purchase price, producer, distributor, rental source, order code number where available, grade level. Descriptive annotation of 10–25 words, based primarily on excerpts from distributors' content summaries.

Special Features: Directory of distributors.

73. **Films on Oceanography.** 3d ed. National Oceanographic Data Center, Washington, D.C. 20390. 1969. $1. 99p. (Publications C-4, in NODC Catalog series)

Scope: Motion pictures and filmstrips dealing with marine science for use in elementary and secondary school and college, and by the general public. Includes general oceanography and the fields of biology, chemistry, engineering, geology, and physics. 155 titles. Most films are available on free loan.

Arrangement: Classified by subject and then alphabetical by title.

Entries: Title, length, silent or sound, color or b/w, availability information about purchase or loan, interest level, 20–80-word descriptive annotation.

Special Features: Listing of naval districts with addresses; title index.

74. **Films Relating to Communism,** by James A. Cook. Research Institute in Communist Strategy and Propaganda, School of International Relations, University of Southern California, Los Angeles, Calif. 90007. 1965. Apply. 418p.

Scope: A comprehensive, annotated list of 1,000 films of interest to public affairs specialists, historians, teachers, and scholars examining Communist affairs. Included in the subject areas are: China, communism in America, Cuba, espionage, ideologies, NATO, peace and disarmament, propaganda, revolution, SEATO, United Nations, USSR, and World War II.

Arrangement: Section 1, subject index in which titles are listed alphabetically under 62 headings. Section 2, series productions. Section 3, alphabetical title list of 1,000 films, described and annotated. Section 4, directory of sources.

Entries: Title, series title if any, producer, source, date, running time, color or b/w, cost for purchase or rental, 50–200-word descriptive annotation.

Special Features: Availability information; spiral binding.

75. **Folk Music: A Catalog of Folk Songs, Ballads, Dances, Instrumental Pieces, and Folk Tales of the United States and Latin America on Phonograph Records.** U.S. Library of Congress, Reference Department, Music Division, Recording Laboratory, Washington, D.C. Available from the Superintendent of Documents, U.S. Government Printing Office, Washington, D.C. 20402. 1964. 40c. 107p.

Scope: Phonodiscs (78 rpm and 33⅓ rpm) representing a sampling of the best of more than 16,000 phonorecords in the Archive of Folk Song of the Library of Congress. Included in the catalog are 107 phonodiscs (78 rpm) containing 341 titles and 59 phonodiscs (33⅓ rpm) with 899 titles of folk music and tales recorded in the field with portable recording equipment, for sale by the Library of Congress.

Arrangement: Classified by subject with alphabetical list of albums and long-playing titles and alphabetical list of individual titles.

Entries: Title of album and/or phonodisc, editor, number of phonodiscs in album, speed, series number, cost for purchase of album and/or phonodisc, titles of songs, performer(s), collector(s), dates, places, and cost for purchase of individual records, size in diameter.

Special Features: Geographical index.

76. **Foreign Language Audio-Visual Guide,** compiled and edited by Bertha Landers. Landers Associates, P.O. Box 69760, Los Angeles, Calif. 90069. 1961. $2.50. 172p.

Scope: More than 2,000 titles of foreign language instructional films, filmstrips, phonorecords, and phonotapes. The material selected emphasizes grammar, vocabulary, and conversation for grade levels from primary through college, in 12 languages: Arabic, Chinese, French, German, Greek, Hebrew, Italian, Japanese, Latin, Portuguese, Russian, and Spanish. Includes background materials for cultural enrichment in the fields of geography, history, art, music, drama, literature, and industry in the desired language.

Arrangement: Alphabetical by languages, then by type of medium and alphabetical by title under medium.

Entries: Title, language, type and size, grade level, running time, color or b/w, producer/distributor plus address, price, brief content description.

Special Features: List of miscellaneous audiovisual materials, such as flags, games, globes, maps, and charts; illustrations by Robert Cain.

77. **Foreign Language Programmed Materials: 1969,** compiled by A. I. Fiks, Fiks Research Associates and published by the Modern Language Association of America and the American Council on the Teaching of Foreign Languages, 62 Fifth Ave., New York, N.Y. 10011.

1969. 25c. 8p. (ERIC Focus Reports on the Teaching of Foreign Languages series)

Scope: Contains bibliographic-retrieval information concerning 48 programs of foreign-language learning materials "currently available to the educational community and the general public"—17 for French, 15 for Spanish, 6 for German, 3 for Russian, 3 for Latin, and 4 for other languages—from 21 producers.

Arrangement: By language and then alphabetical by title.

Entries: Each entry is divided into 3 parts (a, b, c) which in most cases are 3 lines. First part contains title, producer/distributor code, author, price category; second part contains student level, course objectives, the mode of student response and any special devices needed; third part contains format, price, category of format components, time for completion, number of frames or responses, and "atomy," a quantitative index of the degree to which a program fractionates its content.

Special Features: Some comments on programed materials for learning foreign languages and on the list itself; list of producers and distributors and their addresses; bibliography.

78. **Free Films on Air Pollution.** U.S. Department of Health, Education and Welfare, National Air Pollution Administration. Available from Superintendent of Documents, U.S. Government Printing Office, Washington, D.C. 20402. 1969. 15c. 24p. (Revision scheduled for late 1971.)

Scope: 18 films dealing with the problem of air pollution and what to do about it.

Arrangement: 1 film per page with no discernible ordering.

Entries: Title, 100–50-word description of content, producer, television clearance, length, order number.

79. **Guide to Data Education Films,** by Mary Robek, Michigan State University, and Arthur H. Pike, Norwich University. Available from Society of Data Educators, R2-76 Union, Northfield, Vt. 05663. 1970. $3.25. 64p.

Scope: 550 motion pictures selected to aid teachers of data processing at all levels in learning and teaching about automation.

Arrangement: Divided into 2 sections. Section 1, subject matter index, is arranged by subject keywords, permitting use of an IBM-card procedure to locate films dealing with specific topics. Section 2, film descriptions, is alphabetical by title.

Entries: Title, level(s), source, date, running time, sound or silent, color or b/w, availability information, 10–50-word descriptive annotation, keyword numbers to describe subject matter of film.

Special Features: Directory of film sources; subject identification numbers.

80. A Guide to Films, Filmstrips, Maps and Globes, Records on Asia.
3d ed. The Asia Society, 112 E. Sixty-fourth St., New York, N.Y.
10021. 1964. 87p. *Supplement,* published July 1967. 64p. Both guides
are available for 75c or separately for 50c. Orders under $5 must
be prepaid.

Scope: A highly selected list of more than 300 16mm films, 225
    filmstrips, 105 phonodisc titles or albums, and a section de-
    scribing maps, globes, transparencies, and still pictures on
    Asian peoples and cultures. "Asia here is defined as includ-
    ing all countries from Afghanistan to Japan." Each of the 4
    sections of the guide was prepared by a specialist in the
    type of medium (films, filmstrips, records, maps and globes)
    who worked with the Education Department of the Asia So-
    ciety. The *Supplement* includes a new section on slides.

Arrangement: Arranged in 4 parts, by type of medium. The 3 sec-
    tions of films, filmstrips, and records are then alphabetical by
    country or region followed by an alphabetical list of titles.
    The fourth section on maps and globes lists the types, gen-
    eral characteristics, user sources, and series titles for each
    type of medium.

Entries: Title; series if any; producer or distributor; running time;
    date; b/w or color; silent or sound; size of map or globe;
    rpm, size, and number of phonodiscs; and brief descriptive
    annotation.

Special Features: An introduction by the specialist/compiler for
    each type-of-medium section: filmstrips, by Violet M. Bell,
    New York; films, by Melvin E. Levison, Brooklyn College;
    phonodiscs, by William L. Purcell, Wistar Institute Library,
    Philadelphia, and critic, *American Record Guide;* maps and
    globes, by Richard F. Viet, geographer, Westfield, N.J.

81. Guide to Films on International Development, by Jean Marie Ackermann. Film Sense, Box 783, Claremont, Calif. 91711. 1967. $2.50
prepaid; $3 billed. 53p. Apply for quantity discount.

Scope: A collection of 19 of the author's articles which critically
    review 130 films on international development. The reviews
    first appeared in the *International Development Review* and
    are cumulated and reprinted in this separate publication with
    permission of the journal. A listing of source indentifications
    of several thousand films on the subject.

Arrangement: Individual films are grouped according to broad topics,
    described, and evaluated in the 19 critical commentaries which
    are written in literary and narrative style. Bibliographical data
    for films follow each review.

Entries: Title, length, 10–15-word description of content, producer,
    distributor and address, price, reviews of 100–300 words each.

Special Features: Alphabetical index to film titles; geographical index to film titles; film lists on special subjects—Africa, Asia, international development, international understanding and United Nations, Latin America, and Middle East; bibliography of selected readings.

82. **Guide to Films (16mm) about Famous People.** Serina Press, 70 Kennedy St., Alexandria, Va. 22305. 1969. $5.95. 206p. Apply for quantity discount.
    Scope: More than 1,450 16mm films concerning, in whole or part, the lives, times, works, or activities of more than 1,180 famous or well-known, contemporary and historical, persons.
    Arrangement: Alphabetical by title.
    Entries: Title, producer, distributor, running time, color or b/w, 20–50-word descriptive annotation, grade level if available.
    Special Features: Name index; supplemental index of films; producer index; source index.

83. **Guide to Films (16mm) about Negroes.** Serina Press, 70 Kennedy St., Alexandria, Va. 22305. 1970. $3.95. 86p. Apply for quantity discount.
    Scope: More than 740 films dealing with the lives, culture, history, and problems of Negroes in the United States and Africa. Subject areas include: racial discrimination and prejudices; ghetto life; ancient cultures of Africa; civil rights movement; militancy and black power; segregation and desegregation; political, economic, and social developments in Africa; prominent Negroes, past and present, e.g., Martin Luther King, Jr., Stokely Carmichael, Marcus Garvey, Huey Newton, Booker T. Washington.
    Arrangement: Alphabetical by title.
    Entries: Title, source, running time, date if available, color or b/w, 20–100-word descriptive annotation, grade level if available.
    Special Features: Subject index; source index.

84. **Guide to Foreign-Government Loan Film (16mm) in the United States.** Serina Press, 70 Kennedy St., Alexandria, Va. 22305. 1969. $4.95. 133p. Apply for quantity discount.
    Scope: More than 3,000 films available on loan in the United States from 68 foreign governments, 1,800 on a free-loan basis and 1,200 with a nominal fee. Many films with dialogue and/or narration in French, Spanish, Portuguese, Czech, Polish, and Vietnamese languages. Subject areas include: art, customs and cultures, international relations, history, literature, music, science, sports, travel, etc.
    Arrangement: Alphabetical by name of country and then alphabetical by title.

Entries: Title, running time, color or b/w, 20–50-word descriptive annotation.

Special Features: Instructions for borrowing films precede the listing of films from each country; population, area, and capital are given for each country.

85. **Guide to Free-Loan Training Films (16mm).** Serina Press, 70 Kennedy St., Alexandria, Va. 22305. 1970. $5.95. 205p. Apply for quantity discount.

Scope: Approximately 1,950 films available for public, nonprofit exhibition on a free-loan basis. An aid to schools, business, and industry in locating films pertaining to a wide range of subjects. Subject areas include: agriculture, architecture, handicrafts, atomic energy, automation, automotive, aviation, business, carpentry, communications, construction, cooking, creativity, fire control, food and drugs, forests, gas, home economics, hydraulics, maps and mapping, marine fishing, materials handling, measurement and gauging, metals, minerals and mining, noise, occupations, optical, petroleum, photography, physics, plumbing, printing, railroads, refrigeration, research, safety, space technology, synthetic materials, testing, typography, water, welding, writing, miscellaneous.

Arrangement: Alphabetical by subject areas and then alphabetical by title.

Entries: Title, source, running time, color or b/w, 20–50-word descriptive annotation.

Special Features: Title index; source index.

86. **Guide to Government-Loan Film (16mm).** Serina Press, 70 Kennedy St., Alexandria, Va. 22305. 1969. $4.95. 130p. Apply for quantity discount.

Scope: More than 2,000 films of general and professional interest available from governmental agencies.

Arrangement: Alphabetical by governmental agency and then alphabetical by title.

Entries: Title, date, running time, color or b/w, sound or silent, 20–50-word descriptive annotation.

Special Features: General information and instructions for borrowing government-produced films precede the listing of films from each governmental agency; alphabetical title index; alphabetical subject index.

87. **Guide to Military-Loan Film (16mm).** Serina Press, 70 Kennedy St., Alexandria, Va. 22305. 1969. $4.95. 149p. Apply for quantity discount.

Scope: More than 1,430 motion pictures available on loan for public, nonprofit exhibition, free of charge from U.S. Army, U.S. Air Force, U.S. Navy, U.S. Marine Corps. Subject areas include:

air defense, arctic and antarctic regions, career guidance, career opportunities, democracy, drug abuse, foreign countries, missiles, missions of governmental activities, national and world affairs, oceanography, research and development, sports, submarines, Vietnam, U.S. history, weather, World War II.

Arrangement: By series number under specific military branch.

Entries: Series number, title, date if available, running time, color or b/w, 10–30-word descriptive annotation.

Special Features: Source index for each military branch; title index; subject index.

88. Guide to State-Loan Film (16mm). Serina Press, 70 Kennedy St., Alexandria, Va. 22305. 1969. $2.95. 56p. Apply for quantity discount.

Scope: More than 540 films produced by or available from 60 official state agencies in 43 states and the District of Columbia. State agencies which do not lend out of state have been omitted. Most films are available free of charge, but occasionally a nominal service charge is made. Subject areas include: conservation, sports and recreation, fish and wildlife, historic sites and personalities, travel, hunting and fishing, economic development, highways, fire prevention.

Arrangement: Alphabetical by state and then alphabetical by title.

Entries: Title, running time, color or b/w, 20–50-word descriptive annotation.

Special Features: Source for borrowing films for each state.

89. Harrison Tape Catalog: 8-Track, Cassettes, Open-Reel. Cumulative catalog published bimonthly. M. and N. Harrison, Inc., 274 Madison Ave., New York, N.Y. 10016. $1 per single copy; $5 per yearly subscription. (Generally available at record and music shops. Available from M. and N. Harrison, Inc., as a special accommodation only.)

Scope: Approximately 1,400 old and new tapes in 8-track cassettes, and open-reels under such headings as: popular, folk, jazz, shows, films, TV, operetta, Hawaiian, international, religious, spoken, humor, language lessons, children's, classical, opera, vocal, electronic music.

Arrangement: Divided into 2 major sections—section 1, cassettes and 8-track cartridges, and section 2, open-reels. Each section opens with "what's new" and continues with the cumulative catalog for that section, which is divided according to subject (or content) headings. Within each subject category entries are alphabetical, with the type of entry determined by type of tape: popular tapes, by performers; shows and films, by title; classical works, by composers; performances, by solo instrument and orchestra, the soloist's name first and then the conductor's; when a tape includes more than one major work, this information follows a double slash; major works are cross-indexed.

Entries: Performer, composer, soloist; title; format code; company; tape order number; price.

90. An Index of Media for Use in Instruction in Educational Administration, compiled by John J. Horvat. The University Council for Educational Administration, 65 S. Oval Dr., Columbus, Ohio 43210. 1965. $1.25. 58p.

Scope: 319 titles including 156 phonotapes, 107 films, 9 filmstrips, 6 slide sets, 4 phonodiscs, 7 transparency sets, 5 items of programed materials, and 25 other materials compiled through a questionnaire survey. Intended as an aid to those teaching educational administration. Broad subject areas include: tasks of administration, administrative processes and organizational variables, societal factors influencing education, preparation programs for educational administrators, and materials relevant to the area of higher education.

Arrangement: Grouped according to type of medium under broad subject headings, which are divided into more specific subject categories and then media are listed alphabetically by title.

Entries: Title; short description if available; speaker, author, or producer; running time for films and phonotapes; source code.

Special Features: Introductory description telling how questionnaire survey was conducted; source index.

91. Index to Computer Assisted Instruction, edited by Helen A. Lekan. 2d ed. Copyrighted by Instructional Media Laboratory, The University of Wisconsin—Milwaukee. Available from Sterling Institute, 3750 Prudential Tower, Boston, Mass. 01299. 1970. $19.50. 295p.

Scope: A listing of 910 computer-assisted instructional programs in school subjects ranging in level from primary to college and adult education. Designed as an availability resource for persons interested in computer-assisted instruction research and development. Information provided for each program should make it possible for users to initiate communication and possible cooperation with the program developers, which is the basic objective of the *Index.* Includes 55 subject areas: accounting, anthropology, art, astronomy, biology, business, chemistry, Chinese, communication, computer operations and programing, computer systems and utility programs, demography, demonstrations and games, economics, education, engineering, English, foreign languages, French, geography, geology, German, guidance and counseling, health professions, history—English, history—U.S., home economics, international relations, Japanese, Latin, library science, management, mathematics, music, philosophy, physics, political science, programed instruction, psychology, reading, Russian, science, social sciences, social studies, social welfare, Spanish, speech pathology and audiology, spelling, statistics, student opinion survey, system planning, tactical training, technical training, visual perception, vocational rehabilitation. If supplementary equipment is needed, it is specified in the program description.

Arrangement: Alphabetical by subject and then by title.

Entries: Title, author, source, description, prerequisites, level of instruction, type of student, average completion time, logic of program, use of program, supplementary equipment/materials, status of program, availability of program, funding/sponsoring agent, descriptive literature, language of the program, central process or terminal description.

Special Features: Introductory section describes the Instructional Media Laboratory at the University of Wisconsin—Milwaukee and the Sterling Institute; listing of new computer-assisted instruction organizations and related activities; subject index; central processor index; programing language index; instructional logic index; source index.

92. **Index to 8mm Motion Cartridges,** prepared by National Information Center for Educational Media, University of Southern California, Los Angeles, Calif. 90007. R. R. Bowker Co., 1180 Avenue of the Americas, New York, N.Y. 10036. 1969. $19.50 postpaid in the U.S. and Canada. 402p.

Scope: An index to approximately 8,900 individual titles of commercially produced standard-8mm and super-8mm sound and silent motion-picture cartridges compiled from information stored in the NICEM data bank. A significant percentage of the films appeared originally as 16mm and therefore are older than the date indicated. The films range in level from preschool through elementary, secondary, college, and adult audiences, and include the following broad subjects: agriculture, biography, business and economics, civics and government, education, English language, fine arts, foreign language, geography, guidance, health and safety, history, home economics, industrial arts, literature, mathematics, physical education, psychology, religion and philosophy, natural and physical sciences, social science, and sociology.

Arrangement: Main section, the "Alphabetical Guide to 8mm Motion Cartridges," lists individual titles (including all previous editions available) together with series titles, arranged by computer alphabetizing; the section called "Subjects Guide to 8mm Motion Cartridges" lists individual cartridge titles alphabetically (only latest edition) under 26 main subject headings and 397 subheadings.

Entries: Individual cartridge entries, main section: title, size and physical description, length in minutes, stock or color code, description of content, audience or grade level, producer, distributor, and some production credit codes, year of release, and Library of Congress card number (when available).

Series entries, main section: title, version or edition, description of series content, producer, distributor, and production codes, year of release, list of individual titles in series with length in minutes for each title, and Library of Congress card number (when available).

Subject guide entries: title (for films, but not series titles), audience or grade level, and distributor code.

Special Features: "How to Use This Index," "Subject Heading Outline," "Index to Subject Headings," "Directory of Producers and Distributors," part 1, arranged alphabetically by code and including addresses; part 2, arranged alphabetically by name.

93. Index to Overhead Transparencies, prepared by National Information Center for Educational Media, University of Southern California, Los Angeles, Calif. 90007. R. R. Bowker Co., 1180 Avenue of the Americas, New York, N.Y. 10036. 1969. $22.50 postpaid in the U.S. and Canada. 582p.

Scope: Approximately 17,000 individual titles of commercially produced transparencies are included, ranging in grade level from preschool through college, university, and adult audiences. Like those used in the companion NICEM indexes, these titles are those stored in the computerized data bank and include the following broad subjects: agriculture, geography, business and economics, civics and government, education, English language, fine arts, foreign language, geography, guidance, health and safety, history, home economics, industrial arts, literature, mathematics, physical education, psychology, natural and physical sciences, social science, and sociology. Almost all titles are described as "prepared transparency," but there are also a few transparency "masters," "operable" transparencies, and "polarized" transparencies—terms which are all defined in the introduction.

Arrangement: Main section, the "Alphabetical Guide to Overhead Transparencies," includes individual and series titles arranged by computer alphabetizing. The section entitled "Subject Guide to Overhead Transparencies" lists transparency titles alphabetically under 26 broad subject headings and 363 subheadings, omitting earlier editions and out-of-print titles.

Entries: Individual transparencies, main section: title, size and physical description, number of overlays, stock or color code, description, series title (when applicable), audience or grade level, producer and distributor codes, and year of release.

Series entries, main section: title, version or edition, description, producer and distributor codes, year of release, list of individual titles in the series with number of overlays for each.

Subject guide entries: titles of transparencies and series, audience or grade level, distributor codes.

Special Features: "How to Use This Index," "Subject Heading Outline," "Index to Subject Headings," "Directory of Producers and Distributors," part 1, arranged alphabetically by code and including addresses; part 2, arranged alphabetically by name.

94. **Index to 16mm Educational Films,** prepared by National Information Center for Educational Media, University of Southern California, Los Angeles, Calif. 90007. 2d ed. R. R. Bowker Co., 1180 Avenue of the Americas, New York, N.Y. 10036. 1969. $39.50 postpaid in the U.S. and Canada. 1111p. (A supplementary third edition is in preparation and is to be published by NICEM at $18.50.)

Scope: Approximately 27,400 titles of 16mm educational motion pictures (almost all with optical sound) are indexed in this revised edition, an expansion by some 13,000 entries of the first edition published in 1967. Like its predecessor, the second edition was compiled from information stored in the NICEM data bank and includes films on the following subjects: agriculture, biography, business and economics, civics and government, education, English language, fine arts, foreign language, geography, guidance, health and safety, history, home economics, industrial arts, literature, mathematics, physical education, psychology, religion and philosophy, natural and physical sciences, and sociology. The films range from preschool through elementary, secondary, college, university, adult, professional (law, medicine, etc.), industrial, religious, teacher, and special audience levels.

Arrangement: Main section, the "Alphabetical Guide to 16mm Films," includes individual titles and series titles, arranged by computer alphabetizing; the section entitled "Subjects Guide to 16mm Films" lists titles alphabetically under 26 broad headings and 399 subheadings, except for the following omitted titles: those superseded by a later edition; titles which are out-of-print repetition of multireel titles which are listed in the main section both as a single entry and again by part, "for the convenience of libraries in the production of catalogs" (Introduction).

Entries: Individual film entries, main section: title, edition or version, length, stock or color code, audience or grade level, description of content, series title (when applicable), producer, distributor, and production credit codes, date of U.S. release, and Library of Congress card number (when available).

Series entries, main section: title, version or edition, producer, distributor, and production credit codes, list of individual titles in series with running time for each, audience level, and description of content included for some series.

Subject guide entries: title (for films but not series titles), audience or grade level, and distributor code.

Special Features: "How to Use This Index," "Subject Heading Outline," "Index to Subject Headings," "Directory of Producers and Distributors," part 1, arranged alphabetically by code and including addresses; part 2, arranged alphabetically by name.

95. **Index to 35mm Educational Filmstrips,** prepared by National Information Center for Educational Media, University of Southern California, Los Angeles, Calif. 90007. 2d ed. R. R. Bowker Co., 1180 Avenue of the Americas, New York, N.Y. 10036. 1970. $34 postpaid in the U.S. and Canada. 872p. (A supplementary third edition is in preparation and is to be published by NICEM at $12.)

Scope: Approximately 24,500 filmstrips with and without sound and captions are included in this revised edition, an expansion by some 14,500 entries of the first edition published in 1968. The 1970 edition, like its predecessor, was compiled from information stored in the NICEM data bank and includes filmstrips on the following subjects: agriculture, biography, business and economics, civics and government, education, English language, fine arts, foreign language, geography, guidance, health and safety, history, home economics, industrial arts, literature, mathematics, physical education, psychology, religion and philosophy, natural and physical sciences, and sociology. The filmstrips range in level from preschool, through elementary and secondary school, to college and adult audiences.

Arrangement: Main section, the "Alphabetical Guide to 35mm Filmstrips," includes individual titles and series titles arranged by computer alphabetizing; the section entitled "Subject Guide to 35mm Filmstrips" lists titles alphabetically under 26 main subject headings and 397 subheadings. Omitted from this section are titles out-of-print or superseded by new editions. Duplication of titles occurs in the case of filmstrips issued in more than one length (number of frames).

Entries: Individual filmstrips, main section: title, physical description, edition or version, length in frames, stock or color code, audience or grade level, content description, series title, producer, distributor and production credit codes, date, and Library of Congress card number (when available).

Series entries, main section: title, version or edition, producer, distributor, and production credit codes, content description of series, and individual titles in series with number of frames for each.

    Subject guide entries: title, including some series titles, audience or grade level, and distributor code.

Special Features: "How to Use This Index," "Subject Heading Outline," "Index to Subject Headings," "Directory of Producers and Distributors," part 1, arranged alphabetically by code and including addresses; part 2, arranged alphabetically by name.

96. **Instructional Materials for Adult Business and Distributive Education.** University of the State of New York, State Education Department, Bureau of Continuing Education Curriculum Development, Albany, N.Y. 12224. 1969. Apply. 73p.

    Scope: Approximately 630 films, filmstrips, transparencies, charts, phonotapes, and phonodiscs intended to help the business and distributive education instructor stimulate interest and make the learning process more meaningful. Subject headings include: accounting and bookkeeping, banking and finance, business and economics, business skills, consumer education, distributive education, industrial management, insurance, law, office machines, personnel management, stenography, transportation, typing, and vocational guidance.

    Arrangement: Alphabetical by subject headings. Subject headings are subdivided by medium and titles are alphabetical under appropriate medium.

    Entries: Title, producer, date if available, running time or number of frames, silent or sound, color or b/w, distributor code, 10–30-word descriptive annotation.

    Special Features: Producer/distributor code index; alphabetic list of producer/distributors; suggestions on using audiovisual materials.

97. **Instructional Materials for Teaching the Use of the Library,** by Shirley L. Hopkinson. 4th ed. Claremont House, 231 East San Fernando St., San Jose, Calif. 95112. 1971. $1.50 plus 14c postage. 64p.

    Scope: An annotated, selected list of films, filmstrips, phonotapes, charts, books, tests, transparencies, and other aids most of which have been produced since 1960 and designed to aid in teaching library use at elementary school, high school, and college level. 39 motion pictures and 113 titles of individual filmstrips or series of filmstrips.

    Arrangement: Grouped into 5 categories according to medium, then alphabetical by title or author.

    Entries: Title; author or creator; producer/publisher; date; running time; number of frames, pages, or items in the set; b/w or color; price; source; series; guide or manual; grade level; brief annotation summarizing content.

Special Features: Directory of producers, publishers, and other sources.

98. **JEA Media Guide: A National Guide to the Choice of Audiovisual Titles for Use in the Study of Modern Communications,** prepared by the National Curriculum Commission of the Journalism Education Association, Chairman, T. Jan Wiseman, Kishankee College, Malta, Ill. 60150. Newsfoto Publishing Co., San Angelo, Tex. 76901. Available from Mrs. Sara Greer, 103 W. Greer St., Honea Path, S.C. 29654. 1966. 15c. 31p.

Scope: Motion pictures, slides, study prints, and phonodiscs selected for use in the study of modern communications. Only those titles which received excellent or good ratings are annotated. The remainder, considered to be of limited value, are listed separately under the heading related films. Subjects included in the annotated list are: theory of communications, the role and history of mass media, research, mass media and the mass audience, informative writing, persuasion, and communications technology. 140 annotated motion pictures, 8 sets of slides and study prints, 61 related films, and 23 annotated phonodisc albums, which are listed under the subject headings: communicating information, and persuasion.

Arrangement: Annotated and recommended motion pictures arranged by title (but not alphabetically) under broad subject headings. Related films are in a separate section, as are phonodiscs, arranged under subject area.

Entries: Title, producer/source, running time or number of slides or phonodiscs, color or b/w, rating, 30–80-word descriptive annotation.

Special Features: List of film producers and sources.

99. **Landers Film Reviews,** published by Landers Associates, P.O. Box 69760, Los Angeles, Calif. 90069. June 1956 to date. $35 per year. Monthly except July and August.

Scope: Comprehensive reviews of 60 to 70 current 16mm films each month in all subjects, including instructional, documentary, avant-garde, television documentary, industrial message film, American and foreign short subjects, children's fiction films, and other general interest, nontheatrical films, covering releases of approximately 600 producers with new producers added frequently. Reports on award-winning films in American and foreign film festivals. Listing of new multimedia materials: super-8mm sound films, filmstrips, 8mm silent loops, overhead transparencies, disc and tape recordings added in volume 15 (1970) as a monthly service.

Arrangement: 8½" x 11" loose-leaf sheets, with film reviews arranged in alphabetical order in each issue, numerical paging

by the volume (June through September). Subject and title
indexes in each issue, cumulated indexes by the volume.

Entries: Title, distributor, producer, date, running time, color or
b/w, cost for purchase or rental, interest level, descriptive
and evaluative review in 150–200 words.

Special Features: Loose-leaf binder furnished with subscription, 10
monthly issues to be inserted by volume and issue number;
new source directory once a year, with up-to-date addresses
of producers and distributors.

100. Learning Directory 1970–71. Westinghouse Learning Corporation,
100 Park Ave., New York, N.Y. 10017. 1970. $90. 7v.

Scope: First annual edition of a work intended by the Corporation
to be "the comprehensive guide to instructional materials in
all media." The *Directory* includes 205,000 different "intrin-
sically instructional" items which are currently available and
which range in format from books and maps through films,
filmstrips, microforms, multimedia kits, and computer-assisted
instruction programs. Omitted are literature and nonfiction
lacking specific pedagogical emphasis (with some exceptions),
reference works (with some exceptions), entertainment films,
tests, audiovisual equipment, and school supplies. Curriculum
subjects range from all fields of academic study to vocational
training, and the audience levels range from preschool through
college and adult. The data in the "Instructional Materials
Index" were obtained from selected trade catalogs of 618
publishers, producers, and exclusive distributors as well as
from a few major secondary sources. Included within the first
3 categories are selected government agencies, associations,
philanthropic and religious organizations, manufacturers and
other business enterprises which sponsor or produce materials
intended for educational use. Among the 205,000 items included, approximately 23,000 are 16mm films, 8,000 are 8mm
films, and 90,000 are books. Approximately 1,000 sources of
materials are represented.

Arrangement: Volume 1, introductory material on the uses of the
Directory; the "Source Index" arranged alphabetically by the
name of the publisher, producer, or distributor; and the beginning of the "Instructional Materials Index," which is the
main body of the *Directory* and is arranged alphabetically by
topic from the letter A through the letters BOUN. Volumes 2
through 7 contain the remaining parts of the "Instructional
Materials Index," also arranged alphabetically by topic and
divided as follows: volume 2, letters BOUQ through DROS;
volume 3, letters DROU through GREE; volume 4, letters GREG
through MARI; volume 5, letters MARK through PISC; volume
6, letters PISE through SMEL; volume 7, letters SMER through
Z, figures 0–9.

Entries: Topic; audience level, if included in source catalog; type of medium; title; color or b/w; sound; size; running time; number of frames, pages, sides, or reels; date if given in source catalog (if not, *p69* or *p70* is used to designate prior publication); price; free, loan, and purchase options; shortened name of source with reference to catalog and page where item is described; additional notes in coded form.

Special Features: "How to Use the Learning Directory" and "Source Index"; telephone-directory format with yellow pages, paperbound volumes in a slipcase; keyword topic indexing which provides both specific and general subject headings; listing of each item under several subject headings, in many cases; inclusion of tear-out postal cards in each volume for sending comments, suggestions, or corrections to the Westinghouse Learning Corporation and for requesting further information or catalogs from the original sources of the materials.

101. Library of Congress Catalog: Motion Pictures and Filmstrips. Washington, D.C. 1953 to date. Quarterly with annual and quinquennial cumulations. Sent without cost to all subscribers to the *National Union Catalog,* but may be ordered separately. $25. *Motion Pictures and Filmstrips,* 1953–57 cumulation, issued as v.28 of the *National Union Catalog.* $20. 1088p. *Motion Pictures and Filmstrips,* 1958–62 cumulation, issued as v.53, 800p., and v.54, 402p., of the *National Union Catalog.* $20 per v. Quinquennial volumes prior to 1963 are for sale by Rowman and Littlefield, Inc., 84 Fifth Ave., New York, N.Y. 10011. The 2-volume cumulation for 1963–67 is sold by J. W. Edwards, Inc., Ann Arbor, Mich. 48106. $45. Current issues, quarterly with annual cumulation, available from Library of Congress, Card Division, Building No. 159, Navy Yard Annex, Washington, D.C. 20541.

Scope: All motion pictures and filmstrips of educational or instructive value released in the United States or Canada and cataloged on Library of Congress printed cards. Data supplied largely by film producers or distributors. Entries are being prepared for selected television and theatrical films which have been added to the Library's collection.

Arrangement: Alphabetical by title, with producer and detailed subject index including *see* and *see also* references, except for the 2-volume quinquennial issues for 1958–62 and 1963–67 in which the first volume contains only main titles under producers and other added entries; the second volume is a subject index to titles in volume 1.

Entries: Title, motion picture or filmstrip, distributor, producer, author and title of published work upon which the film is based or with which it is correlated, date, running time or number of frames, silent or sound, color or b/w, availability of teacher's guide, series, credits, suggested subject headings. Library of Congress card number, Dewey Decimal Classification number (discontinued in November 1963 and resumed October 1967), descriptive annotation in 15–50 words.

Special Features: Entries also available in card form with *see* and *see also* references provided; current issues contain index of producers and distributors, with addresses.

102. **Library of Congress Catalog: Music and Phonorecords.** Washington, D.C. 1953 to date. Semiannual with annual cumulations at $20. *Music and Phonorecords,* 1953–57 cumulation, issued as v.27 of the *National Union Catalog.* $20. 1049p. *Music and Phonorecords,* 1958–62 cumulation, issued as v.51 and v.52 of the *National Union Catalog.* v.51, $20. 1049p.; v.52, $20. 514p. *Music and Phonorecords,* 1963–67 cumulation, issued in 3v., $75. Quinquennial volumes for 1953–57 and 1958–62 are for sale by Rowman and Littlefield, Inc., 84 Fifth Ave., New York, N.Y. 10011. Quinquennial volumes for 1963–67 are for sale by J. W. Edwards, Inc., Ann Arbor, Mich. 48106. Current issues and annual cumulation available from the Library of Congress, Card Division, Building No. 159, Navy Yard Annex, Washington, D.C. 20541. The next quinquennial cumulation will cover the years 1968–72; therefore, there will be no annual cumulation for 1972.

Scope: Music scores intended for performance and sound phonorecords, musical and nonmusical. The nonmusical recordings cover all subject fields currently received by the Library of Congress and other American libraries participating in its cooperative cataloging program. Books about music and librettos have been included since 1963.

Arrangement: Alphabetical by composer or author, with subject index including *see* and *see also* references, except that volume 51 is an author list, and volume 52 is a subject index to volume 51.

Entries: Composer or author, title main entries, type of medium, publisher or source, catalog number, date, physical description of record giving speed and size, series title, performers, author of program notes, suggested subject headings, Library of Congress card number, Library of Congress Classification number, number of pages, illustrations, size.

Special Features: Entries also available in card form.

103. **Media for Christian Formation,** edited by William A. Dalglish. George A. Pflaum, Publisher, 38 W. Fifth St., Dayton, Ohio 45402. 1969. $7.50. 393p.

Scope: Approximately 350 films, filmstrips, posters, phonodiscs, and phonotapes dealing with such subjects as: citizenship, civil rights, community, courage, culture, dating, education, faith, family, friendship, God, health, justice, love, mankind, marriage, nature, poverty, religion, sex, social problems, values, and war.

Arrangement: Alphabetical by title.

Entries: Title, series title, length or number of frames, type of medium, color or b/w, guide, producer, date of production, distributor, rental rate, rating from *Audio-Visual Resource Guide (AVRG)* and/or *Media for Christian Formation (MCF),* reference to annotations in *Short Films in Religious Education* by William Kuhns and/or National Center for Film Study Guides, 50–150-word description of content, grade level, teaching purposes.

Special Features: Listing of titles by medium; index to distributors and addresses; index to religious and secular film, filmstrip, and tape libraries; subject index.

104. Mediated Teacher Education Resources, edited by W. C. Meierhenry. American Association of Colleges for Teacher Education, 1 Dupont Circle, Washington, D.C. 20036. 1970. $1.50. 67p.

Scope: Approximately 170 audiotapes, gaming and simulations, motion pictures, multimedia, slides and filmstrips, and videotapes designed to aid the teacher educators in preservice and inservice programs.

Arrangement: Alphabetical by type of medium and alphabetical within medium by title.

Entries: Title, producer/distributor, 10–20-word description of content, color or b/w, running time, sale and rental cost, supplemental materials if available.

Special Features: Definitions of terms; list of distributors; names and addresses of AACTE committee.

105. Medical and Surgical Motion Pictures: A Catalog of Selected Films. 2d ed. American Medical Association, 535 N. Dearborn St., Chicago, Ill. 60610. 1969. Free. 572p.

Scope: Approximately 4,800 films intended for those concerned with education of medical students, interns, residents, physicians in all specialties, and those in fields allied to medicine. Subject areas include: basic sciences—anatomy, embryology, genetics, pathology, pharmacology, and physiology; clinical medicine and surgery—anesthesia, cardiovascular surgery, dermatology, gynecology, internal medicine, neurology, neurosurgery, obstetrics, ophthalmology, orthopedic surgery, otorhinolaryngology, pediatrics, physical medicine, preventive medicine, psychiatry, radiology, colon and anorectal surgery, general surgery, thoracic surgery, and urology; paramedical sciences—civil defense, first aid, health careers, history of medicine, hospitals, hospital personnel, medical legal, medical technology, nursing, physical therapy, psychology, public relations and general, socioeconomics, and x-ray technology. The AMA expresses no opinions on the merits of these films, except those reviewed in its *Journal.*

Arrangement: Alphabetical by title within subject categories.

Entries: Title, type of medium, color or b/w, sound or silent, running time, production date, language if other than English, author, distributor, 10–60-word descriptive annotation.

Special Features: Subject index; title index; distributor index.

106. Mental Health Film Guide, compiled by the National Medical Audiovisual Center, Atlanta, Ga. 30333. April 1969. Free. 69p.

Scope: Approximately 385 titles dealing with mental health. Inclusion does not mean endorsement by Public Health Service or U.S. Department of Health, Education and Welfare.

Arrangement: Alphabetical by title.

Entries: Title, producer, date, running time or number of frames, sound or silent, color or b/w, type of medium, accompanying materials, language, series reference, 10–50-word descriptive annotation.

Special Features: Source index.

107. Mental Retardation Film List, prepared by National Medical Audiovisual Center, Atlanta, Ga. 30333. 1968. Free. 60p.

Scope: Approximately 150 films for use in mental retardation education programs. Titles are divided into 2 groups, nonprofessional and professional. Nonprofessional titles deal with the nature of mental retardation—its causes, general treatment, and prevention—and are intended for use by the general public. Professional designates films concerning more specific aspects of diagnosis, clinical treatment, rehabilitation, and control.

Arrangement: Alphabetical by title under professional or nonprofessional category.

Entries: Title, producer, country of origin, date, running time, film size, sound or silent, color or b/w, 20–100-word descriptive annotation, series reference.

Special Features: Title index; distributor index.

108. MLA Selective List of Materials for Use by Teachers of Modern Foreign Languages in Elementary and Secondary Schools, edited by Mary J. Ollmann. Modern Language Association of America, 60 Fifth Ave., New York, N.Y. 10011. 1962. $1.50. 162p. *1964 Supplement for French and Italian.* 1964. $1. 70p. *1964 Supplement for German, Norwegian, Polish, Russian, and Swedish.* 1965. $1. 69p. *1964 Supplement for Spanish and Portuguese.* 1964. $1. 55p. The *Supplements* were prepared under the direction of John T. Harmon by the staff of the Materials Center.

Scope: A selected list of approximately 2,500 items in the main volume and the *Supplements,* including phonodiscs, phonotapes, films, filmstrips, and slides, as well as basic texts, periodicals, maps, and teachers' guides in 10 languages: French, German, Italian, modern Hebrew, Norwegian, Polish, Portuguese, Russian, Spanish, and Swedish. Designed for use by modern foreign-language teachers in elementary and secondary schools, but most categories are considered to be quite useful in college teaching as well. Committees of teachers assisted the staff of the Center in the evaluation of the materials.

Arrangement: By language, then type of medium, and then alphabetical by title. Sets of materials that include films or filmstrips, recordings, and printed matter are listed under the heading integrated programs.

Entries: Title, producer/distributor or author, number of tapes, frames, pages or units, size (mm, rpm, ips), running time, disc serial number, color or b/w, date, grade level, rating by the evaluators, a 20–60-word critical annotation.

Special Features: Selective, descriptive, annotated bibliography of books about the "six cultures": French, German, Hispanic, Italian, Luso-Brazilian, and Russian; description of the criteria used in the evaluation of each type of material; list of sources.

109. **Motion Pictures and Slide Films,** compiled by Department of Education, National Association of Real Estate Boards, 155 E. Superior St., Chicago, Ill. 60611. 1968. Single copies, free; in quantity, $22 per 100. 47p. (Revision scheduled for late summer 1971)

Scope: Approximately 200 titles of films, filmstrips, and slides dealing with the following subjects: advertising, architecture, construction, communication, finance, free enterprise, home ownership, housing, insurance, real estate, sales training, urban/suburban planning, and renewal.

Arrangement: Alphabetical by title with a subject index.

Entries: Title, medium format (films, filmstrips, or slides), length or number, color or b/w, sound or silent, 50–100-word description of content, purchase and/or rental information including source, address, and cost.

110. **National Center for Audio Tapes Catalog. 1970–72.** National Center for Audio Tapes, University of Colorado, Stadium Building, Boulder, Colo. 80302. 1970. $4.50 within U.S.; $5.50 to foreign countries. 123p. 1971 *Supplement.* 46p. $1 within U.S.; $2.50 to foreign countries.

Scope: Approximately 12,000 tapes in main volume selected on the basis of curricular relevance and production quality which can be re-recorded for any individual, group, educational institution, or business firm provided that the restrictions are adhered to. Subject areas include: the arts—general, architecture, dance, drama, graphic art, handicrafts, design, music, painting, photography, printing, and sculpture; education—history, theory and practice, media, and special areas of education; mathematics and science—mathematics, biological sciences, chemistry, physics, geology, meteorology, astronomy, medicine, and space exploration; physical and recreational activities; social studies—history, economics, political science, sociology, anthropology, geography, philosophy, religion, psychology, and military science; vocational and technical fields—engineering, agriculture, business, domestic science, and trades. Policies, procedures, and fees which govern availability and use are given.

Arrangement: Alphabetical by broad subject headings with series titles under subheadings and individual titles under series titles.

Entries: Library of Congress Classification number, series title, Library of Congress card number, grade level, series stock number, series description, producer, date, broadcast restrictions, individual stock numbers, individual titles, running time.

Special Features: General information on arrangement of catalog; purchasing information; producer index.

111. **National Directory of Safety Films, 1969–1970.** National Safety Council, 425 N. Michigan Ave., Chicago, Ill. 60611. 1970. $3.50. 62p.

Scope: More than 1,000 16mm films, sound filmstrips, and 2″ x 2″ slides covering safety in areas of industry, motor transportation, traffic, home, farm, public, and school.

Arrangement: Alphabetical by title under broad subject categories.

Entries: Title, producer, sponsors, distributors, screening time, silent or sound, color or b/w, television clearance, information about purchase or loan, descriptive annotation of 10–40 words.

Special Features: Title index; guide to film sources.

112. **National Medical Audiovisual Center Catalog.** National Medical Audiovisual Center, Station K, Atlanta, Ga. 30324. Available from Superintendent of Documents, U.S. Government Printing Office, Washington, D.C. 20402. 1970. $1.25. 106p.

Scope: Includes approximately 1,000 motion pictures, filmstrips, videotapes, audiotapes, and slide sets dealing with some aspect of a medical or health-related problem area. The intent is that these instructional media will assist in the fulfillment of national teaching and learning objectives. Subjects include: accidents and accident prevention, addiction, administration, agriculture, allergy, anatomy and physiology, anesthesiology, audiovisual aids and materials, autopsy and embalming, biology, body as a whole, cancer, cardiovascular system, chemistry, child care and maternal welfare, civil defense and disaster, cytology and tissue culture, dentistry, digestive system, embryology, evolution, genetics, heredity, endocrine system, environmental health, eye, first aid, gerontology, hemic and lymphatic systems, hospital and medical facilities, human development, human relations, integumentary system, international health, medical and paramedical profession, microbiology, migrant population, military medicine, musculoskeletal system, neurology, nursing and patient care, personal hygiene, pharmacology and toxicology, physical fitness, psychiatry and psychology, radiology, rehabilitation, respiratory system, scientific communications, speech, surgery, urogenital system, veterinary medicine, zoology.

Arrangement: Alphabetical by title in the main entry section. Alphabetical by title under subject headings in the subject index.

Entries: Title, producer, date, length or number of frames, film size, rpm or ips, sound or silent, color or b/w, type of medium, 20–100-word technical descriptions of content frequently including production credits.

Special Features: Borrowing instructions and order forms.

113. Neurological and Sensory Disease Film Guide 1966, prepared by the Public Health Service, Audiovisual Facility for the Neurological and Sensory Disease Service Program, Division of Chronic Diseases, U.S. Department of Health, Education and Welfare, Washington, D.C. 20201. Available from the Superintendent of Documents, U.S. Government Printing Office, Washington, D.C. 20402. 1966. $1.50. 220p. (Public Health Service Publication no.1033)

Scope: Most of the 1,348 titles listed are 16mm motion pictures, a few are filmstrips and slide sets, selected primarily to help medical and allied professional teaching institutions, hospitals, and other users to find educational material related to the field of medicine. The list is comprehensive with no attempt to screen or select qualitatively. Among the 29 neurological diseases included are: cerebral palsy, epilepsy, mental retardation, and speech disorders. Sensory diseases of the ear, eye, larynx, nose, and speech are included.

Arrangement: Alphabetical by title under subject. Title listing.

Entries: Title, producer, country of origin, date if available, running time and/or number of frames when a filmstrip, sound or silent, color or b/w, language versions when other than English, credits, availability information about sale or loan, 20–100-word descriptive annotation for most titles or citation to review.

Special Features: Distributor listing.

114. New Educational Materials, compiled by Mary L. Allison. Citation Press, 50 Forty-fourth St., New York, N.Y. 10036. 1970. $3.75. 256p. 1969 edition, $3. 240p.; 1968 edition, $3.25. 256p.; 1967 edition, $3.25. 256p. No duplication in editions.)

Scope: Annotated listing of films, phonodiscs, phonotapes, multi-media kits, books, filmstrips, transparencies, film loops, tapes, laboratory kits, charts, and maps for the classroom teacher from prekindergarten through the twelfth grade. Each guide contains approximately 500 titles. Subject areas include: language arts, social studies, science, English, the Negro in America, art, music, health, sex, and safety. Many of the evaluations included have been previously published in *Scholastic Teacher* during the school year. Evaluations are made by panelists who are specialists in the subject areas and age levels for which the products have been prepared.

Arrangement: Organized by general type of material and grade level, and classified by broad subject areas and then alphabetical by title. No index.

Entries: Title; author, publisher, or producer; date; price; pages, length, size, or number of frames; grade level; color or b/w; teacher's guide; handbook; initials of reviewer; and 25–750-word evaluative annotation.

Special Features: A section especially for the teacher; a section on references and guides; alphabetical listing of *Scholastic Teacher*'s Evaluation Service panelists; and alphabetical listing of sources of educational materials plus mailing address.

115. **99+ Films on Drugs,** edited by David O. Weber. Educational Film Library Association, Inc., 17 W. Sixtieth St., New York, N.Y. 10023. (Originally published by the University of California, Berkeley) 1970. $3. 68p.

Scope: Approximately 100 films on drugs and narcotics for use with groups from elementary school through college, adult, and professional levels. Includes such subjects as: depressants, community action, pharmacology, drug culture, drug education, hallucinogens, heroin, opium, morphine, legal drug use, marijuana, drug research, amphetamines, and speed.

Arrangement: Alphabetical by title.

Entries: Title, production date, length, color or b/w, distributor, producer, 125–250-word content descriptions, 100–50-word evaluations, overall rating of effectiveness, grade level with target audience level underlined.

Special Features: Description of the drug film evaluation project at the University of California under a grant from the Maurice Falk Medical Fund on which this publication is based; "Substance Abuse in Perspective" by Henry B. Bruyn; "From 99 Reviews—New Perspectives" by C. Cameron Macauley; "A Statement" by the chairman of the Teenage Drug Film Review Committee; a listing of films classified according to overall effectiveness rating; an index classified according to subject headings; series listing; additional drug films not viewed by the Committee; additional drug films currently unavailable; distributor index; EFLA publications list.

116. **Our American Heritage: Audio-Visual Materials Grades K–14.** Cooperative Project of the Office of the Los Angeles County Superintendent of Schools and the school districts in Los Angeles County. Available from the Office of the County Superintendent of Schools, Los Angeles County Schools, Los Angeles, Calif. 90015. September 1962. Free. 92p.

Scope: Approximately 550 titles of films, tapes, recordings, and art reproductions which comprise a representative list of materials having potential for nurturing the development of concepts relevant to our American heritage. Titles were selected from Los Angeles County Board of Education adoption lists. Intended as a teacher's source and guide to help find appropriate and effective materials. Major subject areas included are: roots, growth, and interpretations of our American heritage, as expressed through citizenship and government, lives of our people, our symbols and documents, events and places, and the arts.

Arrangement: Alphabetical by subject and then alphabetical by title.

Entries: Title, catalog number, type of medium, running time, grade level, 20–100-word descriptive annotation.

Special Features: Introduction for each section which gives a general overview and correlates the materials within that area.

Authors' Note: A companion volume listing books for elementary schools and following the same subject arrangement to facilitate the integrated use of media dealing with concepts related to the American heritage is also available.

117. **Police Film Guide,** by Allen P. Bristow. 2d ed. Police Research Associates, P.O. Box 1103, Walteria, Calif. 90505. 1968. $5. 72p.

Scope: Approximately 500 films, filmstrips, and slides dealing with such subjects as: auto theft, civil defense, communism, crowd control, first aid, forgery, legal procedure, narcotics, physiology, race relations, and traffic. Data in the guide are based on replies to a survey made by the author.

Arrangement: Alphabetical by title.

Entries: Title, type of medium, sound or silent, color or b/w, length, number of frames or slides, 20–30-word description of content, producer, numbers referring to distributor(s).

Special Features: Subject-heading index with titles listed alphabetically under appropriate headings; alphabetical list of distributors with addresses.

118. **Programmed Instruction Guide,** compiled by Instructional Technology Information Center, Office of Educational Resources, Northeastern

University, Boston, Mass. 2d ed. Published by Entelek, Inc., Newburyport, Mass. 01950. 1968. $14.50. 400p. (Third edition scheduled for fall 1971. Format will be essentially the same as second edition.)

Scope: A computer-based catalog of 2,221 programs in such subject categories as: philosophy, religion, social sciences, language, science, technology, arts, literature, geography, and history.

Arrangement: By a 4-part number comprised of the entry number, the group designation or subgroup number, the unit number, and the total unit number or supplementary material code numbers. Divided into 2 principal sections, the subject categories index and the data bank printout. Individual programs retrieved by use of a program record sheet and the 4-part unit number.

Entries: Program identification number, title, author or editor, teacher's manual, test type, teaching device, subject matter, content of the program classified using a modified Dewey decimal system, program source (publisher, distributor, or author), assessment data, program style, length of time required to complete program, target population, cost, availability, publication date.

Special Features: Recommendations for reporting the effectiveness of programed instruction materials; bibliography listing bibliographies of programed materials published since 1965; listing of periodicals dealing with programed instruction; listing of names and producers of devices required for the presentation of programs; alphabetical listing of producers with their addresses; instructions on how to locate appropriate programs; subject categories listing; 12 program-record sheets for use in locating desired programs, 4 request cards; different-colored papers to designate 3 major sections.

119. **Programmed Learning: A Bibliography of Programs and Presentation Devices,** compiled by Carl Hendershot with the assistance of publishers, writers, and the National Society for Programmed Instruction. 4th ed. Available from Carl Hendershot, 4114 Ridgewood Dr., Bay City, Mich. 48706. 1968. $11.50; with *Supplements* to late 1970, $27. 700p.

Scope: A listing of programs in school subjects ranging in level from preprimary to college and adult education. The basic publication includes listings to February 1967. *Supplements* describe new releases to late 1970. The few programs which require devices are identified and information regarding devices is provided in a separate section. Multimedia-based instruction and educational systems, which include learner-paced instruction, are described in the *Supplements.* Later *Supplements* include a special grouping of nonprogramed but individually paced instruction.

Arrangement: Divided into 3 sections. Section 1 is an alphabetical list of subjects with program titles included under the appropriate headings. Section 2 is arranged alphabetically by publisher with titles under names of their publishers. Section 3 describes the machines and is arranged alphabetically by manufacturer.

Entries: Subject, title, author, approximate hours, level, number of frames, publisher, cost, availability, machine or device, brief descriptive note indicating prerequisities, possible uses, teacher's manuals, tests.

Special Features: Directory of publishers and manufacturers with code for abbreviations used; a reference list of books and periodicals about programed learning and its use in business, industry, government, schools, and colleges; vinyl binder with index.

120. Psychological Cinema Register: Films in the Behavioral Sciences Catalog, 1967, 1968, 1969; *Supplement* . . . 1969 (bound together), by Psychological Cinema Register, Pennsylvania State University, University Park, Pa. 16802. 1969. Free. 104p. *Supplement,* 20p. Irregular, with supplements appearing between issues. (Revised edition scheduled for 1971)

Scope: Motion pictures in areas of psychology, psychiatry, and other behavioral sciences both popular and scientific in nature, currently available. International. Available for purchase or rental or both. Films reviewed by the editor of the *Psychological Cinema Register* and accepted in consultation with faculty members of the Pennsylvania State University.

Arrangement: Alphabetical by title with indexes to subjects and authors-advisers.

Entries: Title, catalog number, distributor, authors and advisers, sponsoring agency, date, running time, silent or sound, color or b/w, cost for purchase and rental, restrictions on showings, 25–125 word descriptive and evaluative annotation.

Special Features: Information for producers who wish to submit films to *Psychological Cinema Register* for listing; statement of *Psychological Cinema Register* business policy, purchase and rental procedure, and special procedure for foreign purchases.

121. A Quick Reference List of Recent Films Adaptable to the Teaching of Nursing Subjects, by Lucy C. Perry. Rev. ed. Indiana University School of Nursing, Indianapolis, Ind. 46202. Spring 1970. $1.50. 28p.

Scope: Approximately 300 recent films related to the teaching of nursing subjects to assist faculty members and graduate students preparing to teach. Categories listed are: accidents and accident prevention, addiction, anesthesiology, audiovisual communication, aviation medicine, biology, body as a whole, cardiovascular system, child care and maternal welfare, communications, dentistry, digestive system, ear, endocrine system, environmental health, eye, first aid, gerontology, hospital and medical facilities, integumentary system, international health, medical and paramedical profession, microbiology-epidemiology, military medicine, musculoskeletal system, neurology, nursing and patient care, nutrition, obstetrics, personal hygiene, pharmacology and toxicology, physical fitness, psychiatry and psychology, radiology, rehabilitation, respiratory system, social problems, speech, surgery, urogenital system, and zoology. Films are available from film libraries which do not charge a fee other than the cost of return postage.

Arrangement: Classified by subject category and then alphabetical by title.

Entries: Title; distributor; call number if available; running time; production date if available; silent or sound; color or b/w; no annotation but if the title does not give a clue to content, a phrase in parentheses follows the film title to clarify it.

Special Features: List of 36 film library sources.

122. **Railroad Film Directory,** compiled by the Association of American Railroads, American Railroads Building, Washington, D.C. 20036. 12th ed. 1969. Apply. 48p. Frequently revised.

Scope: Motion pictures and filmstrips owned by or relating to American railroads, including films which feature the history, physical properties, operations, and accomplishments of the railroads, and many films which feature agricultural and industrial developments as well as recreational and scenic attractions in the United States and Canada. Approximately 325 titles.

Arrangement: Alphabetical by title under type of medium with subject index.

Entries: Title, distributor and producer, running time, silent or sound, color or b/w, availability on free or rental basis, television clearance, narrative phonorecords or study guides (if any), descriptive annotation of 15-30 words.

Special Features: Address list of railroads, industry sponsors, and commercial distributors from whom films may be obtained; railroad and subject index.

123. **Recordings for Children: A Selected List,** prepared by New York Library Association, Children's and Young Adult Services Section. 2d ed. Available from New York Library Association, P.O. Box 521, Woodside, N.Y. 11377. 1964. $1. 43p.

Scope: A highly selected cross section of the best recordings available with stress on those best suited for the home and recreational collection. Includes folk music, rhythms and games, dances, patriotic songs and marches, camp songs, foreign languages, documentaries, science, religion, Shakespeare words and music, Christmas music, classical and contemporary music, and nonmusical recordings—spoken records of poetry and folk and fairy tales. Most of the phonodiscs are 33⅓ rpm, but the few 78 rpm that are still available have been included. Approximately 500 entries.

Arrangement: Alphabetical by album title under subject heading.

Entries: Album title, composer/author, performing group, narrator, producer/recording company, record number, and a brief description.

Special Features: Asterisk indicates suggested "first purchase" except in classical and contemporary music.

124. References on Foreign Languages in the Elementary School, by Elizabeth Keesee. Office of Education, U.S. Department of Health, Education and Welfare, Washington, D.C. 20201. Available from the Superintendent of Documents, U.S. Government Printing Office, Washington, D.C. 20402. 1963. 40c. 49p. (Circular no.495, revised)

Scope: Motion pictures, phonodiscs, filmstrips, slides, pictures, games, teachers' guides, and supplementary readers and children's books useful in teaching French, German, Spanish, Russian, Italian, and Hebrew in the elementary school.

Arrangement: Classified by individual foreign languages, then by medium, and then alphabetical by title.

Entries: Title; distributor; production date; running time or number of frames for films and filmstrips; color or b/w for films and filmstrips; number, speed, and size in diameter for phonodiscs; cost of purchase; availability of accompanying teacher's guides and phonodiscs for filmstrips; descriptive annotation of 10–25 words.

Special Features: Professional materials, such as books, bulletins, and reports; language journals and services for teachers; addresses of publishers, phonorecord producers, and film distributors in the United States; addresses of importers and distributors.

125. Retail Training Film Directory. Rev. ed. Personnel Group, National Retail Merchants Association, 100 W. Thirty-first St., New York, N.Y. 10001. 1968. Members, $5; nonmembers, $7.50. 66p.

Scope: More than 200 films covering a wide variety of subjects and intended as an aid in training retail employees. Subject headings include: home furnishings, ready-to-wear and accessories, men's wear and men's furnishings, textiles, miscellaneous merchandise, miscellaneous subjects, sales training, general, office and restaurant store operations, supervisory training, retail careers, and recordings.

Arrangement: Alphabetical by subject areas and then alphabetical by title.

Entries: Title; distributor; type of medium; running time; 10–60-word descriptive annotation; terms of borrowing, renting, or buying film.

Special Features: Descriptions of the characteristics of the visual training aids included in the *Directory;* guidelines for selecting training aids and preparing the presentation; title index; distributor index.

126. Schwann Record and Tape Guide. Monthly. *Schwann Supplementary Record Guide.* Semiannual. W. Schwann, Inc., 137 Newbury St., Boston, Mass. 02116. Available in some 3,800 record shops in the U.S. and in 38 foreign countries. (If unavailable locally, apply to publisher for a list of dealers who solicit subscriptions.)

Scope: Formerly *Schwann Long Playing Record Catalog,* the title was changed in 1971 to reflect the addition of prerecorded 8-track cartridge and cassette tapes to this monthly list of approximately 35,000 currently available 33⅓ rpm phonodiscs. Issued on 770 labels, the phonodiscs include: classical, popular, jazz, rock, folk, and electronic music; ballet, opera, and musical shows. Tapes were added to the popular music section in February 1971, and other listings will be added until every musical category will include tape listings. The *Schwann Supplementary Record Guide,* published in fall and spring, includes many records not listed in the monthly *Guide,* including older popular, imported, spoken, and monorecords.

Arrangement: Alphabetical by composer, followed by his works listed alphabetically by title. Other sections list new releases. Subject and type-of-record categories, with marginal headings in boldfaced type.

Entries: Composer, birth, and death dates; title; opus and part number; conductor/artist; date; producer; order code number; monaural or stereo; and disc or tape.

Authors' Note: A first reissue reprint of the entire Schwann *Catalog* October 1949–December 1969 is available as a 19-reel 35mm positive microfilm from AMS Press, Inc., 56 East 13th St., New York, N.Y. 10003, or Berkeley St., London W.1, England; in each issue there is a column describing recent books on music; an advertising index; and the following separate lists based on information in the monthly *Guide* and *Supplementary Guide: The 1970 Artist Issue Schwann Catalog* of classical long-playing records designed to be used with the monthly publication, particularly the May 1970 issue since the classical records included in these 2 publications are the same except for method of listing (in one by performer, in the other by composer and title). Published at 3-year intervals and available at local record stores, or directly from the publisher at $2.25 postpaid; *1970–71 Country and Western Tape and Record Guide* available at record stores or directly from publisher at $1 postpaid; *Schwann Children's Record Guide,* 1970, published annually and if not available from local dealer, may be ordered directly from publisher for 35c postpaid; *The Schwann Basic Record Library,* arranged by musical periods, available free from the publisher upon receipt of a stamped, self-addressed, no.10 envelope.

127. Selected Audio-Visual Aids for Traffic Engineers. Institute of Traffic Engineers, 2029 K St., N.W., Washington, D.C. 20006. 1965. Free. 26p. (*Supplement* scheduled for publication in 1971)

Scope: Approximately 100 selected motion pictures, filmstrips, and slide sets useful to traffic engineers and other professionals concerned with highway transportation. The directory was developed from a review of more than 500 units of audiovisual materials.

Arrangement: Alphabetical by title.

Entries: Title, type of medium, length or number of frames or slides, sound or silent, color or b/w, production date, 10–30-word description of content, organization and address from which the particular aid is most likely to be available.

Special Features: Supplementary pages for additions to the directory, especially listings published in *Traffic Engineering* magazine; detachable pages designed for recommending additions to the listing.

128. A Selected Discography of Solo Song, by Dorothy Stahl. Information Coordinators, Inc., 1435–37 Randolph St., Detroit, Mich. 48226. 1968. $2.50. 90p. 1968–69 *Supplement.* 1970. $2.50. 95p.

Scope: 1,657 titles (835 in first volume and 822 in the *Supplement*) of recorded art songs in the standard repertoire and a few concert arias sung by great singers. Russian songs, complete operas, and oratorios have been omitted.

Arrangement: Alphabetical by composer and under composer, alphabetical by title.

Entries: Song title, name of artist, the title of the recording or an abbreviation of it as indicated in the Schwann *Catalog,* the record number, and item number in this publication. Stereo recordings are either underlined or placed in parentheses.

Special Features: Index of song titles and first lines in one alphabetical listing; index to abbreviations used on record labels; list of recordings indexed.

129. Selected Drug Abuse Education Films. National Clearinghouse for Drug Abuse Information, 5454 Wisconsin Ave., Chevy Chase, Md. 20015. Available from Superintendent of Documents, U.S. Government Printing Office, Washington, D.C. 20402. 1970. 10c. 12p. (A comprehensive film catalog is scheduled for publication by National Clearinghouse for Drug Abuse Information.)

Scope: 13 films suggested for use by junior and senior high school classes studying drug abuse and/or the general public concerned with the nature, treatment, and control of drug addiction or with the broader social issues such as poverty, inner-city life, and the alienation of youth.

Arrangement: Alphabetical by title.

Entries: Title, producer, distributor, date of production, length, b/w or color, sound or silent, purchase price, target audience, 150–200-word description of content.

Special Features: Suggestions for using films; loan request forms.

130. Selected Films and Filmstrips on Food and Nutrition. Committee on Evaluation of Food and Nutrition Films and Filmstrips. Food and Nutrition Council of Greater New York, Inc., Teachers College Press, Teachers College, Columbia University, New York, N.Y. 10027. 1961. $1.50 (including *Supplement*). 72p. *Supplement.* 1964. 14p.

Scope: A selected list of films covering food and nutrition. A few of the subject divisions included are: career guidance, child feeding, community health, dental health, food budgeting, gardens, industry, food preparation, general nutrition, overweight, physiology, pregnancy and infant feeding, teaching methods, and world food problem. 140 entries.

Arrangement: The 1961 edition is in 2 parts—films and filmstrips— each alphabetical by title under broad subject headings. The *Supplement* includes both films and filmstrips in 1 section, alphabetical by title under broad subjects.

Entries: Title, producer, distributors, date, sound or silent, color or b/w, length or number of frames, audience, 40–100-word description, appraisal.

Special Features: Source and availability information; members of the Committee on Evaluation, 1948–64; alphabetical title indexes of films and filmstrips, including brief subject classification and audience suitability.

131. Selected Films: Heart Disease, Cancer, and Stroke, compiled by National Medical Audiovisual Center, Atlanta, Ga. 30333. Rev. ed. February 1968. Free. 76p.

Scope: Approximately 150 titles of selected films on heart disease, cancer, and stroke.

Arrangement: Alphabetical by subject, which is further divided into professional and nonprofessional levels and then alphabetical by title.

Entries: Title, producer, distributor, date, running time, sound or silent, color or b/w, 30–100-word descriptive annotation.

Special Features: Distributor index; subject index.

132. Selected Films on Child Life. Rev. ed. Children's Bureau, Office of Child Development, U.S. Department of Health, Education and Welfare, Washington, D.C. 20201. Available from the Superintendent of Documents, U.S. Government Printing Office, Washington, D.C. 20402. 1965. 40c. 114p. (Children's Bureau Publication, no.376)

Scope: 480 16mm films which were reviewed by the professional staff of the Children's Bureau and considered to be a value for adult audiences, although listing does not constitute endorsement. Also included are a few films which were made for classroom use with children. Reprinted in 1969, this catalog supersedes all previous listings. Some of the subjects included are: adolescents, adoption, alcohol, amputees, baby sitting, blindness, cerebral palsy, child care, child health, child study, children of other countries, deafness, emotionally disturbed children, family life, juvenile delinquency, handicapped children, maternity care, mental retardation, preschool children, recreation and play, safety, sex education, and speech defects.

Arrangement: Alphabetical by title.

Entries: Title; producer; date; screening time; sound or silent; color or b/w; availability through free loan, rental, or purchase; suggested audience; 20–60-word descriptive annotation.

Special Features: Subject index; directory of distributors.

133. Selected Free Materials for Classroom Teachers, by Ruth H. Aubrey. Rev. ed. Fearon Publishers, 6 Davis Dr., Belmont, Calif. 94002. 1969. $2. 128p.

Scope: More than 2,000 units of free instructional materials from 571 sources including print and nonprint media. With the exception of films, each of the free materials has been examined by one or more of the panel of evaluators on the basis of importance, presentation, usefulness, and freedom from undesirable advertising and bias. Subjects include: agriculture, art, business, conservation, language arts, health, home economics, industrial education, mathematics, music, occupational guidance, physical education, recreation, safety, science, and social science.

Arrangement: Alphabetical by subject and under each subject, alphabetical by source.

Entries: Source, address, title of unit of instructional material, medium format, availability note (quantity, etc.), grade level.

Special Features: Suggestions for ordering free materials; names and addresses of distributors; subject and producer index.

134. Selected List of Audiovisuals: Dentistry. National Medical Audiovisual Center, Atlanta, Ga. 30333. March 1968. Free. 111p.

Scope: Approximately 250 titles including films, filmstrips, slides and kinescopes. Major subject areas included are: anesthesiology, careers, diagnosis and treatment planning, endodontia, materials, oral pathology, oral surgery, orthodontics, periodontia, preventive, prosthetics, radiology, restorative, and oral cancer.

Arrangement: Alphabetical by subject areas and then alphabetical by title.

Entries: Title, producer, distributor, type of medium, date if available, running time, sound or silent, color or b/w, 20–100-word descriptive annotation.

Special Features: Title index; distributor index; subject index.

135. **A Selected List of Recorded Musical Scores from Radio, Television and Motion Pictures,** compiled by James L. Limbacher. 5th ed. Available from the Audio-Visual Division, Henry Ford Centennial Library, 16301 Michigan Ave., Dearborn, Mich. 48126. 1970. $3. 70p.

Scope: Selected list of recorded musical scores, limited to scores especially composed for films and does not include musical comedies or vocal theme songs from either films or television. Many of the recordings listed have become collector's items and are no longer generally available. The specific areas of coverage include: (1) full scores, suites, and themes from feature-length motion pictures; (2) music from short subjects; (3) scores, suites, and themes from television programs; and (4) scores and themes from radio programs. More than 1,600 entries.

Arrangement: Divided into 4 sections under the above-mentioned headings. All sections are arranged alphabetically by title of film or program.

Entries: Title, producing or releasing company (foreign releases are listed by country of origin only), year of original release, composer(s), record number, all records 33⅓ rpm except those noted as 45 or 78 rpm, stereo or monaural versions, complete scores and suites underlined for easy identification.

Special Features: Composer index.

136. **Sex Education Resource Unit—Grades K, 1, 2, 3, 4.** American Association for Health, Physical Education, and Recreation, 1201 Sixteenth St., N.W., Washington, D.C. 20036. 1969. 40c. 24p.

Scope: Approximately 50 films, filmstrips, slides, and transparencies recommended for use in sex education units, grades K through 4.

Arrangement: Alphabetical by title under type of medium, which is subdivided by producers alphabetically arranged.

Entries: Title, color or b/w, purchase cost, rental cost, length or number, 30–75-word descriptive annotation.

Special Features: Suggested aims and objectives of sex education for grades K through 4; selected student references; selected teacher references.

137. **Slides and Filmstrips on Art,** compiled by Vincent Lanier as part of the NAEA-USOE Uses of Newer Media in Art Education Project. National Art Education Association, 1201 Sixteenth St., N.W., Washington, D.C. 20036. 1967. $1. 40p.

Scope: Selected 2" x 2" and 3¼" x 4" slides and filmstrips useful in art education for kindergarten through college and adult levels. The materials accumulated in this catalog are the result of more than 600 letters of inquiry to commercial firms, museums, and other agencies producing and distributing instructional media.

Arrangement: Divided into 2 parts. Part 1 is arranged chronologically for arts of ancient civilization and alphabetically by country for later art. Under individual countries breakdowns by century are given when such indications are significant. Part 2 contains general interest headings classified by type of medium and, within each medium, alphabetically by producer/distributor.

Entries: Title, producer/distributor, number or length, type of medium, cost, brief description of content or titles of individual units in a set for approximately one-fourth of the entries.

Special Features: Key to producers and distributors; key to abbreviations.

138. **Sources of Free and Inexpensive Educational Materials,** by Esther Dever, 4th ed. Esther Dever, P.O. Box 186, Grafton, W. Va. 26334. 1970. $6.30. 538p. Quantity rates on request.

Scope: Approximately 5,000 units of instructional materials including films, filmstrips, slides, phonotapes, booklets, and graphic materials recommended for elementary, junior high school, high school, and adults. Includes several hundred sources of materials for which single items are not listed. Covers such subjects as: agriculture, arts and crafts, atomic energy, auto mechanics, aviation, banking and finance, biology, birds, business, economics, conservation, electricity, forests, gas, health, home economics, industrial arts, mathematics, music, reading, safety, science, social studies, and transportation.

Arrangement: Divided into 2 sections. Section 1 is arranged alphabetically by subject areas, under which sources of instructional materials and their addresses and free and inexpensive materials are given in nonalphabetical order. Section 2 lists producers/publishers and their addresses.

Entries: Producer/publisher, address, catalog number of item, title, type of material, number of slides or length of film, cost. (In many instances only the catalogs of the company are listed.)

139. Space Science Educational Media Resources: A Guide for Junior High School Teachers, edited by Kenneth M. McIntyre, based on a report to the National Aeronautics and Space Administration. Rev. ed. Bureau of Audiovisual Education, University of North Carolina, Chapel Hill, N.C. 27514. 1966. $3.50. 89p. Appendix. 9p.

Scope: 16mm motion pictures and filmclips, filmstrips, flat pictures, transparencies, slides, phonotapes, charts, graphs, demonstration devices, field trips, self-instructional 8mm film loops, and programed materials concerned with space science. Compiled as a teaching resource guide correlated with the *Curriculum Bulletin for Eighth Grade Earth and Space Science* of the North Carolina Department of Public Instruction and with the state-adopted textbook *Modern Earth Science, 1961.* Includes 89 films and 39 filmstrips, along with other newer media and classroom-activity suggestions relevant to each of the 3 space science resource units: earth in space (astronomy), space exploration, and meteorology.

Arrangement: Alphabetical by title within broad subjects included in resource units, under type-of-media headings. Title indexes for films and filmstrips in appendix.

Entries: Title, source (producer or distributor), running time or number of frames, color or b/w. Descriptive/evaluative annotations vary from 1 short sentence to 50 words in length.

Special Features: Suggested principles and activities for each unit of eighth-grade earth science; use of color to distinguish sections of the pamphlet; addresses of producers and distributors for all media listed; list of bibliographies, guides, and miscellaneous publications (such as reprints, current periodicals, and paperbacks) concerned with space science; supplementary list of recently produced motion pictures and 31 filmstrips.

140. Spoken Records, by Helen Roach. 3d ed. Scarecrow Press, Box 656, Metuchen, N.J. 08840. 1970. $7.50. 288p.

Scope: More than 500 spoken recordings, including documentaries, lectures, and interviews; readings by authors (Robert Frost, T. S. Eliot, W. B. Yeats, William Faulkner, and others); readings by other than authors in English, American, Scottish, Irish; children's literature; religious and biblical works; and plays of Shakespeare and others.

Arrangement: By subject categories and then alphabetical by title.

Entries: Title, producer/distributor, size and number of recordings, phonodisc number. A critical annotation is given in the main text.

Special Features: Title index; selected discography of Shakespeare's plays and company addresses of Shakespeare recordings; in addition to the Shakespeare discography there is a basic discography of 40 spoken records selected on the basis of excellence, and described in detail in appropriate chapters; appendix 1, data of historic and human interest which became available during the study of *Spoken Records;* appendix 2, supplementary list of spoken records and addresses of record companies cited.

141. **State Films on Agriculture,** produced by or for state colleges, universities, and state agencies. Motion Picture Service, Office of Information, U.S. Department of Agriculture, Washington, D.C. 20250. 1962. Apply. 86p.

Scope: More than 500 16mm films from land-grant colleges and universities, including the extension services and other state agencies of 30 different states and Puerto Rico. Subjects most extensively covered are: agricultural economics, agricultural engineering, animal diseases, beef cattle, corn, dairying, forestry, 4-H Club and Future Farmers of America, fruit gardening, home economics, nutrition, pests and diseases of plants, poultry, soil conservation, vegetables, wildlife and game. All of the films are available for television, colleges, schools, and various organizations—some for loan within or beyond the producing state, some for previews, and some only for purchase.

Arrangement: Alphabetical by state.

Entries: Title; running time; date; color or b/w; information concerning free loan, sale, or rental; television clearance; brief descriptive annotation.

Special Features: Index of subjects.

142. **Study Materials for Economic Education in the Schools.** Joint Council on Economic Education, 1212 Avenue of the Americas, New York, N.Y. 10036. 1969. $1.50. 70p.

Scope: Approximately 100 films and filmstrips recommended for secondary level economic education including such subjects as: general nature of economics; markets, prices, and resource allocation; income determination, stabilization, and growth; role of government and economic institutions; international economics; comparative economic systems and economic history. Basic selection criteria included: genuine concern with economic matters, analytical in nature, and appropriate for secondary use. Some printed materials are reviewed.

Arrangement: Major content areas subdivided by topic and materials listed alphabetically by title under topics.

Entries: Title, type of medium, author, length or number of frames or pages, color or b/w, publisher or producer and address, production date, subject headings, grade level, analytical concepts ascribed to the unit, 30–50-word description of content.

Special Features: Report on the work of the evaluation committee; alphabetical listing by title categories for materials evaluation report.

143. **Suggested Series of Movies for a Course in Urban Planning,** compiled by Ambrose Klain. Council of Planning Librarians, P.O. Box 229, Monticello, Ill. 61856. 1970. $1. 6p. (Exchange Bibliography 154)
    Scope: 20 motion pictures, all produced since 1962 except *The River* (1939), recommended for an introductory college course in urban planning. Selection was based on ratings by junior and senior college students and the author's value judgments.
    Arrangement: By subject and then alphabetical by title.
    Entries: Title, production date, running time, rating, distributor, rental cost when available, subject, comments.
    Special Features: Tabular format.

144. **Themes—Short Films for Discussion,** by William Kuhns. George A. Pflaum, Publisher, 38 W. Fifth St., Dayton, Ohio 45402. 1969. $9.95. 296p.
    Scope: 112 films dealing with such themes as: apathy, awareness, belief, body, city, communication, community, conformity, freedom, friendship, generation gap, human relations, integration, leadership, loneliness, Negro, poverty, self-discovery, sex, social responsibility, technological society, war, and youth; and on such curricular topics as: art, art history, English, guidance, health, history, social studies, languages, science, and mathematics.
    Arrangement: Alphabetical by title.
    Entries: Title, production date, length, distributor, producer, rental rate, production credits, approximately 1-page description of content, suggested uses, suggested questions.
    Special Features: Loose leaf, hard cover with vinyl binding, heavy paper; numerous full-page stills from the films; addresses of distributors; bibliography; thematic index; curriculum index.

145. **United States Atomic Energy Commission Combined 16mm Film Catalog.** (Supersedes the former *Popular-Level* and *Professional Level USAEC Film Catalogs*) U.S. Atomic Energy Commission, Washington, D.C. 20545. 1970. Free. 80p.
    Scope: Part 1: education-information lists 17 categories, 3 series, and 154 films with indicated interest levels for schools, general public, television stations, colleges and universities; part 2: technical-professional lists 13 categories and 108 films for colleges and universities, industry, researchers, scientists, engineers, and technologists; part 3: historical subjects lists 16 categories, 1 series, and 85 films for schools, general public and professional-technical audiences. 347 total titles. Subjects

include: agriculture, atomic energy, biology, data processing, engineering, fuels, medicine, mining, nuclear weapons, nuclear explosives (peaceful), power reactors, radioisotopes, safety, and uranium prospecting.

Arrangement: Alphabetical by film title under broad subject categories for each of the 3 parts and 5 series.

Entries: Title, producer, production date, running time, color or b/w, television clearance, interest level, availability information for purchase or free loan from 12 domestic film libraries, 50–200-word descriptive annotation.

Special Features: Title indexes for each of the 3 parts; combined title index for all films; U.S. Atomic Energy Commission motion-picture film library locations and service areas; where to purchase prints; how to order; loan requirements; sales source addresses; kept up-to-date by "inserts."

146. **U.S. Atomic Energy Commission 16mm Classroom Films on Nuclear Science.** U.S. Atomic Energy Commission, Washington, D.C. 20545. 1970. Free. 43p.

Scope: 57 films especially selected for their classroom and instructional value from among more than 400 popular and professional-level films in the nuclear science field on the following subjects: general interest, general science, physics, chemistry, and biology. Films represent a number of producers and are available on free loan for educational nonprofit use from USAEC domestic film libraries.

Arrangement: Classified according to 5 subject fields and then alphabetical by title.

Entries: Title, length, color or b/w, date, television clearance, producer, series title, grade level, 100–200-word description of content, suggested readings, availability information for purchase or free loan from 12 domestic film libraries.

Special Features: Introduction to the catalog addressed to the science teacher; title index; U.S. Atomic Energy Commission motion-picture film library locations and service areas; how to order; loan requirements; list of appropriate *Understanding the Atom* booklets and order blank.

147. **U.S. Government Films: A Catalog of Motion Pictures and Filmstrips for Sale by the National Audiovisual Center,** National Archives and Records Service, General Services Administration, Washington, D.C. 20409. 1969. Free. 165p.

Scope: Approximately 2,600 films and filmstrips produced by 23 governmental agencies (not including the Department of Agriculture), which cover "a wide range of knowledge and skills" and "are Federal records, since they document the functions and operations of Federal Agencies." They are classified according to the following subject areas: agriculture, automotive, aviation, business, education, electricity, electronics, health, human relations, machining, marine, medicine, national security, physical fitness, safety, science, social studies, technical, woodworking.

Arrangement: Each section is divided into 2 major sections, films and filmstrips, alphabetical by subject headings and then alphabetical by title within subject headings.

Entries: Title, length or number of frames, sound or silent, color or b/w, 16mm or 35mm, item order number, purchase price, in some instances the producing agency, 25–75-word description of content, and, for medical and some technical films, the educational authors.

Special Features: Film title index; filmstrip title index; general ordering information.

148. **U.S. Government Films for Public Educational Use—1963,** by Seerley Reid and Eloyse Grubbs, with the assistance of Katharine W. Clugston. Office of Education, U.S. Department of Health, Education and Welfare, Washington, D.C. 20202. Available from the Superintendent of Documents, U.S. Government Printing Office, Washington, D.C. 20402. 1963. $3. 532p.

Scope: Motion pictures and filmstrips produced by the U.S. government and currently available for public educational use in many subject fields, such as the prevention of forest fires, the training of military personnel, and the control of communicable diseases. Practically all are available to foreign countries as well as within the United States. Approximately 6,000 titles.

Arrangement: Alphabetical by title with subject index.

Entries: Title, government agency responsible for production, date, running time or number of frames, silent or sound, color or b/w, loan and purchase sources, series title if part of series, order number if any, significant relationship to other films, Library of Congress card number, television availability if so cleared, descriptive annotation of 25–40-words.

Special Features: Key to sources of availability of films and filmstrips; general information about motion pictures and film services of the U.S. government, and their sources.

149. **Urban Outlook: A Selected Bibliography of Films, Filmstrips, Slides and Audiotapes,** compiled by the U.S. Department of Housing and Urban Development. For sale by the Superintendent of Documents, U.S. Government Printing Office, Washington, D.C. 20410. 1969. 45c. 38p.

Scope: Motion pictures, filmstrips, slides, and audiotapes concerning architecture, building codes, housing, new towns, pollution, transportation, and urban renewal. Media listed were produced after 1960. Inclusion does not indicate endorsement. 184 entries in main bibliography and 15 items in HUD Audio Tape Index.

Arrangement: Alphabetical by title within subject categories.

Entries: Title, production date, type of medium, b/w or color, silent or sound, length, number of slides in set or of frames in filmstrip, source with address, rental and/or purchase price or free loan, 25–75-word annotation.

Special Features: Title index; alphabetical list of subject categories in table of contents; HUD Audio Tape Index.

150. **Visual Aids for Business and Economic Education.** South-Western Publishing Co., 5101 Madison Rd., Cincinnati, Ohio 45227. 1969. Apply. 35p. (Monograph no.92)

Scope: Motion pictures, filmstrips, charts, and a few phonodiscs generally available for use in classes in business and economics. Subject areas include bookkeeping, business English, guidance, office machines and office practice, salesmanship and distributive education, shorthand, social business, teacher training, and typewriting.

Arrangement: Classified by subject and type of medium and then alphabetical by title.

Entries: Title, distributor, running time or number of frames, silent or sound, color or b/w, approximate cost for purchase or rental or availability on free loan.

Special Features: Part 1, some fundamental principles for the effective use of audiovisual aids; Part 3, names and addresses of producers and distributors of visual-aid material and equipment; Part 4, reference list.

151. **Water Pollution: A Selected List of Recommended and Related Films,** compiled by Madeline S. Friedlander. Educational Film Library Association, Inc., 17 W. Sixtieth St., New York, N.Y. 10023. 1966. $1. 6p. (EFLA Service Supplement) (Revision scheduled for 1971)

Scope: A selected and recommended list of 16mm films on and about water pollution, including current as well as earlier films, dated in some ways but still useful and relevant as background. Related films deal with contamination of the environment of which water and other kinds of pollution are a part. 28 film entries.

Arrangement: Alphabetical by title under the following headings: recommended films, background films, and related films.

Entries: Title, producer/distributor, date, running time, color or b/w, sound or silent, a 50–150-word descriptive annotation.

Special Features: Directory of sources; list of other EFLA publications; film lists on conservation; names and addresses of sources for additional information and material on water pollution; and suggestions for "stimulating audiences to action."

152. **What's New on Smoking in Print and Films.** Rev. ed. U.S. Department of Health, Education and Welfare, National Clearinghouse for Smoking and Health, U.S. Public Health Service, 5600 Fishers Lane, Room 11-A-45, Rockville, Md. 20852. Available from Superintendent of Documents, U.S. Government Printing Office, Washington, D.C. 20402. 1970. 10c; 100 for $7.50. 12p.

Scope: 18 films and filmstrips on smoking recommended by the National Interagency Council on Smoking and Health as valuable to many audiences, including young and old, smokers and nonsmokers. Areas included are: cancer, heart disease, tuberculosis, and respiratory diseases. Also includes reference to selected printed materials.

Arrangement: Alphabetical by title according to producer/publisher.

Entries: Title, author, length or number of pages, color or b/w, date, 10–40-word description of content.

153. **A Working Bibliography of Commercially Available Audio-Visual Materials for the Teaching of Library Science,** by Irving Lieberman. Occasional Papers, Publications Office, University of Illinois Graduate School of Library Science, Urbana, Ill. 61801. 1968. Free. 77p. Occasional Papers no.94)

Scope: Approximately 533 films, filmstrips, phonotapes, and non-projected graphic materials to be used in conjunction with the teaching of library science. "An updated and revised edition of a bibliography which was originally prepared for the National Conference on the Implications of the New Media for the Teaching of Library Science held at Chicago, Illinois, in 1963 . . . is a working copy—both in content and form . . . does not tend to be either definitive or evaluative."

Arrangement: Alphabetical by title according to 7 categories—introduction to librarianship, reference, use of books and the library, cataloging, book selection, printing, and the history of books.

Entries: Title, distributor or producer, type of medium if not film, date (when available), running time, color or b/w, interest level, and annotation (when available). Annotations are from 20–60 words and are quoted from various sources.

Special Features: Directory of producers, publishers, and other sources; title index; vita of Irving Lieberman.

Professional Organizations in the Educational Media Field

American Library Association (ALA), 50 E. Huron St., Chicago, Ill. 60611. Executive Director, David H. Clift

Membership open to persons interested in extending and improving library service and librarianship in the United States and throughout the world. The understanding and use of newer media are implemented by the Audio-Visual Committee, the Editorial Committee, and the 14 divisions of ALA through research and study, special publications, institutes, and projects. The divisions most directly concerned are the Adult Services Division (ASD), the American Association of School Librarians (AASL) which is also an associated organization of the National Education Association, the Association of College and Research Libraries (ACRL), the Children's Services Division (CSD), the Library Education Division (LED), the Public Library Association (PLA), Resources and Technical Services Division (RTSD), the Young Adult Services Division (YASD), and the Information Science and Automation Division (ISAD).

American Libraries, the official journal of ALA, includes articles, news items, and product information on many library- and media-related subjects as well as ALA organizational news. *The Booklist,* a semimonthly list of materials recommended for library purchase, regularly includes reviews of 16mm and 8mm films, filmstrips, and nonmusic phonorecords. *Choice* and *Choice Reviews on Cards* are monthly book-reviewing periodicals for college libraries issued by ACRL. Another periodical, *Library Technology Reports,* is published bimonthly through the Library Technology Program and provides evaluations of library equipment and supplies tested by independent laboratories. Through its book publishing program, ALA also publishes and distributes standards for audiovisual services prepared by appropriate divisions, such as AASL's *Standards for School Media Programs* (ALA-NEA, 1969) and PLA's *Guidelines for Audiovisual Materials and Services for Public Libraries* (ALA, 1970). In addition, several of the divisions publish membership journals, for example,

College and Research Libraries, Library Resources and Technical Services, School Libraries, Top of the News, the *Journal of Library Automation,* and *JOLA Technical Communications.*

Association for Educational Communications and Technology (AECT), 1201 Sixteenth St., N.W., Washington, D.C. 20036. Executive Director, Howard B. Hitchens, Jr.

A professional organization active in the systematic planning, application, and production of communications media for instruction. Founded in 1923, AECT (formerly the Department of Audiovisual Instruction, NEA) was reorganized in 1970 as a national affiliate of the National Education Association. The general purpose of the Association is the improvement of education and the public welfare through the use of educational communications and technology, media, and audiovisual methods. Under its new constitution AECT is developing divisions representing major educational communications and technology areas of national or international scope; divisions formed as of January 1971 include Telecommunications, Information Systems, Research and Theory, Instructional Development, and Industrial Training and Education.

Regular membership includes subscription to the official AECT monthly magazine, *Audiovisual Instruction (AVI).* A special membership includes the quarterly journal *AV Communication Review (AVCR).* Other types of membership are available for students, retired members, libraries, and businesses. There is also a joint membership with the National Association of Educational Broadcasters (NAEB).

In addition to *AVI* and *AVCR,* members receive the monthly newsletter *ect,* and may use the AECT placement clearinghouse. AECT holds annual conventions and sustains a large publishing program.

Association of Chief State School Audio-Visual Officers (ACSSAVO), President, Ralph Ferguson, Director, Audio-Visual Services, State Department of Public Instruction, 1333 W. Camelback Rd., Phoenix, Ariz. 85013.

Membership includes individual representatives of all state departments of education who, either by office or designation, are in charge of the department's program and activities associated with the use of audiovisual media in schools in the state. Through semiannual meetings and a broad sharing of reports and developments, the Association proposes to contribute to the preservice and in-service education of teachers in the improvement of instruction through mediated learning experiences; to raise the professional requirements for certification of personnel responsible for supervising and administering school audiovisual programs; to improve the quality and quantity of materials, equipment, and facilities available to teachers and students; to serve as liaison between the industry and educators; and to encourage and report innovation and research in the production and use of audiovisual materials and equipment.

Educational Film Library Association (EFLA), 17 W. Sixtieth St., New York, N.Y. 10023. Executive Director, Mrs. Esmé Dick

Membership includes schools, colleges, public libraries, church groups, labor organizations, film producers, distributors, and individuals. Founded in 1943, EFLA serves as the national clearinghouse of information about films including their production, distribution, and use. Since 1946, EFLA has operated a film evaluation service providing users more than 7,000 film evaluations by more than 100 film juries. The evaluations are available in two formats, 3" x 5" cards and books. Since 1958, EFLA has sponsored the American Film Festival and issues annually the *American Film Festival Guide.* It also sponsors film workshops. The official publication is *Sightlines.*

Members receive special monographs and reports, such as *Using Films, Manual on Film Evaluation, Service Supplements,* and film bibliographies on selected topics. They have access to EFLA's extensive reference files and reference services either by phone or in person. The EFLA library is open three days a week for personal reference and research.

The Advisory Service handles time-consuming requests such as research on hard-to-find titles, specialized evaluations, plans for distribution or deposit of prints, and special selected film lists. There is a nominal fee for the service.

Educational Media Council, Inc. (EMC), 1346 Connecticut Ave., N.W. Washington, D.C. 20036. Executive Director, Harriet Lundgaard

The 16 members of the Council are nonprofit national associations or organizations having a substantial concern with educational media and materials. Through its two or three meetings each year, EMC serves its members as a forum for discussion of developments and problems of mutual concern and as an information clearinghouse. The Council undertakes research and dissemination projects which by their nature and scope are beyond the capacity of individual member organizations and which are deemed serviceable to member constituencies and the educational community at large. Among such projects have been sponsorship of the multimedia *Educational Media Index,* compilation of an annual *Directory of Summer Session Courses on Educational Media,* and a study for the U.S. Office of Education on *Educational Media in Programs for the Culturally Disadvantaged and Vocational Education.* From time to time the Council also sponsors conferences and publishes reports on subjects related to advancement and amelioration of the uses of media in education.

Film Library Information Council (FLIC), 17 W. Sixtieth St., New York,

N.Y. 10023. Chairman, Board of Directors, William Speed, Los Angeles Public Library, 630 W. Fifth Ave., Los Angeles, Calif. 90017.

Organized in 1967, the Film Library Information Council identifies as its major purposes those of getting the best, the most stirring, the most provocative films in use at the community level and of working with other material organizations to promote greater film use by libraries. Membership includes film librarians from public libraries and others concerned with promoting community use of films. *Film Library Quarterly* is FLIC's official journal.

Services to members include the journal, an annual meeting, and access to a forum on increasing the usefulness of films in general education.

National Association of Educational Broadcasters (NAEB), 1346 Connecticut Ave., N.W., Washington, D.C. 20036. President, William G. Harley; Executive Vice President, Chalmers Marquis

Serves the professional needs of its various kinds of memberships which include educational institutions, noncommercial radio and television stations, and individuals. NAEB's purpose is to promote the dissemination of information by and about radio and television for educational and cultural purposes. The Educational Broadcasting Institute offers in-service training courses; a personnel placement service is provided; and regional and national conferences are held. Official publications include the monthly *NAEB Newsletter,* the bimonthly *Educational Broadcasting Review,* and special monographs. Joint membership with the Association for Educational Communications and Technology (AECT) is available.

National Association of Language Laboratory Directors (NALLD), Box E, Brown University, Providence, R.I. 02912. Executive Secretary, James W. Dodge

Membership includes anyone whose interests bring him in working contact with the administration or operation of any machine-aided language learning program in an educational institution or governmental agency. Purpose is to promote more effective use and better understanding of the machine-aided learning laboratory in foreign-language programs. *NALLD Journal* is the official publication. The Publications Center is a free service to NALLD members.

National Society for Programmed Instruction (NSPI), Trinity University, 715 Stadium Dr., San Antonio, Tex. 78212.

Membership is open to anyone interested in supporting the purpose of the Society. The primary purpose is the advancement of education through the collection, development, and diffusion of information concerned with the process of programing instruction. The process involves the systematic design of learning environments through successive approximations until the learning reaches optimum relevance and efficiency. Many localities have chapters, and members are invited to join these local chapters. The official publication is the *NSPI Journal.*

University Film Association (UFA), President, John Blair Watson, Director, Audiovisual Center, Dartmouth College, Hanover, N.H. 03755.

Membership of the Association includes writers, editors, directors, cameramen, and technicians producing educational, documentary, scientific, and public relations films in colleges and universities. Purposes include promoting an interest in the training and professionalism of film producers in universities, providing a forum for exchange of ideas among this group and with other groups whose interests relate to film production, screening and evaluating university-produced films, and recording developments and activities in the field. Through its affiliated organization, the University Film Foundation, the Association handles research contracts and provides scholarships and fellowships in the production and improvement of the motion picture as an educational tool. Official publications include *Journal of the University Film Association* and a *Newsletter of the University Film Association.*

Periodicals in the
Educational Media Field—
A Selected List

AHIL Quarterly. American Library Association, 50 E. Huron St., Chicago, Ill. 60611. Quarterly. Membership.

Official publication of the Association of Hospital and Institution Libraries, a division of ALA. Includes news and activities of the Division's officers and committees, reports of meetings, announcements of new publications, and information about federal legislation of concern to the membership. Featured in each issue are book reviews and nonprint reviewing services.

American Record Guide, incorporating the *American Tape Guide.* P.O. Box 319, Radio City Station, New York, N.Y. 10019. Monthly. $4.50.

Articles and critical reviews about monaural and stereo phonodiscs and phonotapes. Reviews of books and some nonmusical phonorecords are included. Section entitled "Sound Ideas" reviews equipment each month.

ASFA Notes. American Science Film Association, P.O. Box 3407, Washington, D.C. 20010. Irregular. Apply.

Newsletter of ASFA. Brief articles concerning the personnel, history, literature, and recent developments in the field of science film production. Brief descriptions of recent motion pictures on scientific topics, with content notes.

Audio. North American Publishing Co., 134 N. Thirteenth St., Philadelphia, Pa. 19107. Monthly. $5.

Addressed to hobbyists and serious students. Articles concerned with installation, construction, and maintenance of audio equipment and new products. Reviews classical, popular, and jazz music and nonmusic phonorecords.

Audio-Visual Communications. United Business Publications, 200 Madison Ave., New York, N.Y. 10016. Bimonthly. $3.

Brief articles, reports, and news items with emphasis on the use of audiovisual media in industrial training, public relations, marketing, and management. Also includes articles and information on the use of media in formal education and in government training programs. Reports new equipment and supplies and descriptively reviews new books and films.

Audiovisual Instruction. Association for Educational Communications and Technology, National Education Association, 1201 Sixteenth St., N.W., Washington, D.C. 20036. Monthly September through May with combined June-July issue (10 issues). Membership (nonmembers $12)

Official publication of AECT addressed to teachers, media specialists, and others concerned with trends and news in the field. A major portion of each issue is devoted to exploring a theme in depth, e.g., media and social concerns, teacher education, managing the information explosion. Includes feature articles in each issue by teachers and authorities in educational technology, reports of AECT activities, reviews of professional literature and also of recently produced media and equipment.

AV Communication Review. Association for Educational Communications and Technology, National Education Association, 1201 Sixteenth St., N.W., Washington, D.C. 20036. Quarterly. $5 per year to members (nonmembers $13)

Official publication of AECT dealing with the theoretical aspects of audiovisual communication. In-depth technical articles concerning research in the use of educational technology and new approaches to learning. Features include book reviews, abstracts of research, and departments on teaching machines, programed instruction, and world communications.

The Booklist. American Library Association, 50 E. Huron St., Chicago, Ill. 60611. Semimonthly (except one issue in August). $12.

Since September 1, 1969, *The Booklist* has published reviews of filmstrips and 8mm film loops, and on September 1, 1970, it added regular sections of reviews of 16mm films and nonmusical recordings (discs, tapes, and tape cassettes). Consultant groups (librarians, teachers, media specialists, and curriculum specialists) cooperate with the staff in evaluating the media which range from preschool to adult levels and are in all subject areas. Consistent with *Booklist* policy, only reviews of items recommended for purchase are published.

Business Screen. Harbrace Publications Inc., 402 W. Liberty Dr., Wheaton, Ill. 60187. Monthly. $3.

Concerned with nontheatrical audiovisual media and equipment for business, industry, government, advertising, and associations.

Feature articles, case histories, and brief notes about new products, applications, personnel changes, new literature, sources of material and information; book reviews, film reviews and regular annual guides to equipment, production services, and audiovisual presentation specialists.

Educational Broadcasting Review. National Association of Educational Broadcasters, 1346 Connecticut Ave., N.W., Washington, D.C. 20036. Bimonthly. Membership (nonmembers $6)

The official journal of the NAEB, published in cooperation with Ohio State University. Includes in-depth articles on significant developments in public broadcasting and in the use of radio and television in formal and informal instruction. Controversies and issues are reported in Open Forum. Other regular departments are Book Reviews, Program Reviews, and Research Reviews including selections from ERIC. (Formerly *NAEB Journal*)

Educational Media. 1015 Florence St., Fort Worth, Tex. 76102. Monthly (except combined July-August issue). $10 to nonqualified subscribers; $1 per issue.

Begun in 1969 and addressed to school administrators, supervisors, teachers, curriculum and media specialists. Articles are drawn largely from experience in the field and describe learning systems, computer-assisted instruction, dial access to videotaped information, the use of computers in automating library processes, and many other uses of equipment and multimedia. Regular departments are Products—Publications—People, Films—Tapes—Records, Washington, Letters, and Forum.

Educational Product Report. The Educational Products Information Exchange Institute, 386 Park Ave. S., New York, N.Y. 10016. Monthly, October–June. $35.

Reports findings of EPIE Institute, a nonprofit membership corporation whose purpose is to develop, correlate, and disseminate impartial evaluations of learning materials, equipment, and systems. During the year subscribers receive 5 major reports, each covering a single product or service in depth and comprising 60 to 80 pages, and 4 interim reports on changing applications, product alterations, studies from curriculum development and research centers, government findings affecting products, and follow-up information on the major reports.

Educational Screen AV Guide. 434 S. Wabash Ave., Chicago, Ill. 60605. Monthly (July-August issue combined). $6.

Editorial comment and articles addressed to the teacher and school media specialist. Departments include film evaluations edited by L. C. Larson, Carolyn Guss, and William Cuttill; "AV in Religion" edited by William S. Hockman; lists of new equipment and new publications; and AV news. A special feature is the "Annual Blue Book," a list of new audiovisual materials, which is published in the July-August issue.

Educational Technology. 140 Sylvan Ave., Englewood Cliffs, N.J. 07632. Monthly. $18.

Research reports and technical papers concerning communications theory, instructional systems, and the innovative uses of software and hardware in education, government programs, and industrial training. A single topic is emphasized in each issue, e.g., performance objectives in education, individualized instruction, teacher education, programed instruction, and the computer in education. Regular departments feature new equipment and materials, news notes, book reviews, and opinions.

Educational Television. C. S. Tepfer Publishing Company, Inc., 607 Main St., Ridgefield, Conn. 06877. Monthly. $8.

Addressed to persons concerned with the productions and use of educational broadcasting in schools and colleges, medicine, business, industry, and the military. Articles written by specialists have covered such subjects as film techniques for educational and instructioned television, medical television, master-antenna TV systems, and ITV cost effectiveness and funding. Regular features include editorials, literature reviews, titles cleared for television, and descriptions of new products.

Film Library Quarterly. Film Library Information Council, 17 W. Sixtieth St., New York, N.Y. 10023. Quarterly. Membership (nonmembers $8)

The official publication of FLIC, organized in 1967. The information and articles are addressed primarily to film librarians in public libraries but are of interest to a much wider audience, particularly the descriptions of film making and biographies of film makers. Signed reviews of books and films provide frank, critical appraisals.

Film News: The International Review of AV Materials and Equipment. Film News Co., 250 W. Fifty-seventh St., New York, N.Y. 10019. Bimonthly. $6.

News of film societies, festivals, and meetings and current developments in the audiovisual field. Descriptive and evaluative annotations of films, filmstrips, and phonodiscs are regularly featured. New Films department provides brief descriptive annotations of most recently produced films.

High Fidelity. Billboard Publications, Inc., 2160 Patterson St., Cincinnati, Ohio 45214. Monthly. $7.

Addressed to the informed enthusiast and collector of high-fidelity phonodiscs and tapes. Includes articles about music and musicians written by well-known musicians and journalists. Provides audio equipment reports based on laboratory tests, information on new trends (e.g., video equipment for amateurs) and critical reviews of classical, folk, jazz, and popular music phonorecords. Published also in regional editions and a combined *High Fidelity/Musical America* edition, monthly at $14; or including "Concert Artist Directory," published in December, $20.

Journal of the SMPTE. Society of Motion Picture and Television Engineers, 9 E. Forty-first St., New York, N.Y. 10017. Monthly. Membership (nonmembers $16)

Official publication of SMPTE. Technical papers, research articles, and abstracts concerning engineering, theory, and standards for the professional producing fields of motion pictures, television, instrumentation, and high-speed photography. Includes book reviews, appraisals of new equipment, announcements of new products, calendar of meetings, employment service, and a journal available/wanted section.

Journal of the University Film Association. Robert W. Wagner, Department of Photography and Cinema, Ohio State University, 156 W. Nineteenth Ave., Columbus, Ohio 43210. Quarterly. Membership (nonmembers $4)

Official publication of UFA. Research reports and technical articles concerned with the theory and practice of film making. Evaluative reviews of nontheatrical motion pictures produced by university film units in the United States.

Library Technology Reports. American Library Association, 50 E. Huron St., Chicago, Ill. 60611. Bimonthly in loose-leaf form. $100.

Official publication of the Library Technology Program, sponsored by ALA. The primary objective of LTP is to explore ways and means by which modern technology and the principles of scientific management can be used to solve some of the administrative problems of libraries. The information in *Library Technology Reports* falls into three categories: impartial and precise reports of individual testing and evaluation of library equipment and supplies; research articles providing systems analyses and market surveys giving information availability and selection criteria for equipment and supplies; and a set of four regular features—Abstracts, Questions and Answers, LTP News, and New Products.

Single issues of the *Reports* are available for $20. Available also is a series of *Portfolios* at $35 each on single topics previously published in the *Reports.* Those include data on tape recorders, photocopiers, record players, microform readers, shelving, card catalog cabinets, and many other topics.

Media & Methods. Media & Methods Institute, Inc., 134 N. Thirteenth St., Philadelphia, Pa. 19107. Monthly (September–May). $5.

Addressed to secondary school teachers and professional school faculties with emphasis on practical and effective methods of using media in the high school classroom. There are 12–15 articles in each issue in the following categories: editorials, teaching and theory; paperbacks; films and media mix; television, records, and tapes. Special departments are: Feedback (letters to the editor), Have You Discovered? (materials review), Recommended Shorts, Earsights, and Audiofile (phonorecord reviews). (Formerly *Educator's Guide to Media and Methods*)

Modern Media Teacher. George A. Pflaum, 33 W. Fifth St., Dayton, Ohio 45402. Bimonthly during the school year (5 issues). $5.

Founded in 1969 and addressed to elementary and secondary school teachers. Most of the articles are teachers' reports of experiences in using or in making instructional materials. Regular features are book reviews, news items, and descriptions of new equipment. A major portion of each issue is a subject list of "New Releases" (films, filmstrips, tapes, study prints) with descriptive annotations and ordering information.

NALLD Journal. Newsletter of the National Association of Language Laboratory Directors. Ohio University, Athens, Ohio 45701. Quarterly. Voting members $6; library subscription $9.

Official publication of NALLD. Articles report developments in teaching methods, software, hardware, and assessments of the state of the art. Reviews, news items, and other information of interest to the profession.

Newsletter. Great Plains National Instructional Television Library, University of Nebraska, Lincoln, Neb. 68505. Monthly (irreg.). Apply.

Official publication of the Great Plains National Instructional Television Library. Brief articles describing new developments in instructional television programing and equipment, and the utilization and administration of recorded television courses in schools and colleges. Highlights developments in kinescope and videotape telecourses, most of which are circulated from the Library.

NIT Newsletter. National Instructional Television Center, Box A, Bloomington, Ind. 47401. Five issues per year, September–May. Apply.

Each issue describes television materials which NIT, a nonprofit organization, develops and makes available to elementary, secondary, higher, and continuing education. Also included are brief news items about activities of the Center and its 3 regional branches.

Notes. Music Library Association, Executive Secretary, 3229 School of

Music, University of Michigan, Ann Arbor, Mich. 48105. Quarterly. Membership (nonmembers $10, institutions $15).

Addressed to music librarians and devoted primarily to book and phonorecord reviews, written and compiled by authorities in the field. Unique feature is the consensus record review which serves as an index to the reviews appearing in 15–20 other periodicals. The opinions of the reviewers are indicated by symbols denoting 3 primary grades of opinion: excellent, adequate, inadequate. *Notes* also includes articles of interest to music scholars, news of developments in recording equipment, cataloging and classification, and problems of copyright.

Now Available. ERIC at Stanford. The Newsletter from the Clearinghouse on Educational Media and Technology, Institute of Communication Research, Stanford University, Stanford, Calif. 94305. Bimonthly. Free.

Each issue lists documents processed or cited by the Clearinghouse and arranged by broad subjects, e.g., television and radio, simulation and gaming, audio recording, film, microteaching, programed instruction. Also includes brief news items, announcements of meetings, new publications, and developments in the field.

NSPI Journal. National Society for Programmed Instruction, Trinity University, 715 Stadium Dr., San Antonio, Tex. 78212. Monthly (except January and August). $12.50 to members (nonmembers $20)

Official publication of NSPI. Scholarly articles and research reports concerning the theory, production, and utilization of programed instructional materials. Brief accounts of recent developments, conferences, and publications. Short, evaluative reviews of published programs.

Preview. NET Film Service and Indiana University Films, Audio-Visual Center, Indiana University, Bloomington, Ind. 47401. Irregular. Apply.

Descriptive listing of current film releases from National Educational Television and Indiana University Films. Complete synopses and content notes, with purchase and rental information.

School Libraries. American Association of School Librarians, American Library Association, 50 E. Huron St., Chicago, Ill. 60611. Quarterly. Membership (Single copies may be purchased from the executive secretary for $2.)

Official publication of AASL, a division of ALA and an associated organization of NEA. Articles of current interest concerned with services, standards, manpower, legislation, materials, methods, and other aspects of media-center administration. Reports trends and activities in the field and news of the organization including the "President's Page" and "From the Secretary's Desk." Critical signed reviews of research, new publications, and professional tools.

School Library Journal. R. R. Bowker, Co., 1180 Avenue of the Americas, New York, N.Y. 10036. Monthly. (September–May) $7. Published also as a part of the *Library Journal* mid-month issue.

Addressed to children's, young adult, and school librarians. Articles of interest on contemporary education, media collections, facilities, personnel, services, and standards. Regular departments include letters, a calendar, an editorial, news, people, a checklist of professional publications, signed critical reviews of professional literature, the audiovisual guide, and brief, signed reviews of new books for preschool through young adult levels.

Sightlines. Educational Film Library Association, Inc., 17 W. Sixtieth St., New York, N.Y. 10023. Five times a year. Membership (nonmembers $8)

Official publication of EFLA. Includes many of the features of the former *EFLA Bulletin* and combines many of the separate EFLA publications into one publication. Cuts across the whole field of the nontheatrical film (16mm, 8mm, and filmstrips). Covers children's films, advanced scientific films, the conventional text-centered classroom film, and the avantgarde experimentalist's films. Some of the regular departments include: News Notes, From the EFLA Office, Publications Roundup, Film Review Digest, Who's Who in Filmmaking, and the Filmlist.

Stereo Review. Ziff-Davis Publishing Company, 1 Park Ave., New York, N.Y. 10016. Monthly. $6.

Feature articles and technical reports devoted to audio equipment and information about music, musicians, and composers. Descriptive-evaluative reviews of classical and popular music and entertainment phonorecords, both phonodiscs and phonotapes, with ratings of artistic performance and quality of stereo recording.

Teachers Guides to Television. P.O. Box 564, Lenox Hill Station, New York, N.Y. 10021. 1 issue per semester. $2.25 for one semester; $3.50 for two semesters.

Provides teacher's guides to the educational utilization of selected upcoming programs of the 3 major networks. Includes synopses, related questions and activities, correlated bibliographies of printed materials prepared by the American Library Association and a nonprint list by Carolyn Guss.

Top of the News. American Library Association, 50 E. Huron St., Chicago, Ill. 60611. Issued November, January, April, and June. Membership.

Official publication of the Children's Services Division and Young Adult Services Division of ALA, featuring not only the Divisions' programs and news but also international events concerning publishing and production of books, magazines, films, phonorecords, and other media for children and young adults. Includes interesting, authoritative articles by leading authors, critics, and librarians; profiles of authors; Newbery and Caldecott medal winners and their runners-up as well as announcements of other national and international children's book and film awards; critical reviews of research and books about literature and reading for children and young adults. Each issue includes one or more highly selected, annotated lists of current books for children and young adults.

Educational Media Catalogs and Lists Published since 1957 but Unavailable in 1971

Annotated Bibliography of Audio-Visual Aids for Management Development Programs. Research Service, P.O. Box 1240, Grand Central Station, New York, N.Y. 10017. 1958. 24p.

Annotated List of Filmstrips for Use with the Deaf, by Patricia Blair Cory. Alexander Graham Bell Association for the Deaf, Inc., Volta Bureau, 1537 Thirty-fifth St., N.W., Washington, D.C. 10007. 1960. 81p.

Audio-Visual Aids for Automation. Bureau of Business and Economic Research, School of Business Administration, San Diego State College, San Diego, Calif. 92115. 1965. 77p. (Superseded by *Guide to Data Education Films,* 1970)

Audio-Visual Aids for International Understanding. World Confederation of Organizations of the Teaching Profession, 1330 Massachusetts Ave., N.W., Washington, D.C. 20005. 1961. n.p.

Audiovisual Aids for Teaching Speech in English and Speech Classes of the Secondary School. The University of the State of New York, New York State Education Department, Bureau of Secondary Curriculum Development, Publications Distribution Unit, Albany, N.Y. 12224. 1958. 32p.

Audio-Visual Media and Materials on Mental Retardation. National Association for Retarded Children, 420 Lexington Ave., New York, N.Y. 10017. 1965. 40p.

Bibliography of Audio-Visual Aids for Courses in American Literature, compiled and annotated by Sister Mary Brian. Rev. ed. National Council of Teachers of English, 508 S. Sixth St., Champaign, Ill. 61820. 1957. 20p.

Bibliography of Films on Aerospace Medicine. National Medical Audiovisual Center, Atlanta, Ga. 30324. 1967. 27p.

Biographies for Junior High: A List of Biographies and Correlated Audiovisual Aids, by Louise Smith Mountz. Reprinted from the *Illinois English Bulletin* and distributed by the National Council of Teachers of English, 508 S. Sixth St., Champaign, Ill. 61820. 1957. 52p.

Books on Magnetic Tape: A Catalog of Tape Recordings Which Supple-

ment the Talking Book Program. Division of the Blind, U.S. Library of Congress, Washington, D.C. 1962. 127p. (Revised edition scheduled)

Cancer Film Guide, 1963. Cancer Control Branch, Public Health Service Audiovisual Facility, U.S. Department of Health, Education and Welfare, Washington, D.C. 20201. 1963. 183p.

Catalog of Selected Films on Pediatrics and Child Health, prepared by the American Medical Association and the American Academy of Pediatrics. American Academy of Pediatrics, 1801 Hinman Ave., Evanston, Ill. 60204 or American Medical Association, 535 N. Dearborn St., Chicago, Ill. 60610. 1959. 52p.

Children's Record Reviews. 677 Jefferson Ave., St. Paul, Minn. 55106. October 1957 to 1966. $10 per year and $2 for cumulative index. Issued 5 times per year. (Published irregularly in 1966; no issues in 1967)

Composite List of Conservation and Related Film Titles. Conservation League, 110 W. Seventieth St., New York, N.Y. 10023. 1966.

Computer-Assisted Instruction Guide. 2d ed. Entelek, 42 Pleasant St., Newburyport, Mass. 01950. 1969.

A Critical Index of Films and Filmstrips in Conservation Dealing with Renewable Resources, Non-Renewable Resources, Resources and People, and Ecology. O'Hare Books, 10 Bartley Rd., Flanders, N.J. 07836. 1967. 79p.

Directory of Geoscience Films. American Geological Institute, 1444 N St., N.W., Washington, D.C. 20005. 1962. 63p. (Revised edition scheduled)

Educational Film Guide, edited by Josephine Antonini. 11th ed. H. W. Wilson Co., 950 University Ave., New York, N.Y. 10003. 1953. 5-year cumulated supplement, 1954–58. Annual supplements, 1959, 1960, 1961, 1962. Ceased publication in 1962.

Farm Film Guide, 1965–1966: A Comprehensive Listing of Films and Filmstrips Relating to All Phases of Agribusiness. Business Screen Magazine, 402 W. Liberty Dr., Wheaton, Ill. 60187. 1965. 49p.

Film Guide for Industrial Training. National Metal Trades Association, 222 W. Adams St., Suite 1463, Chicago, Ill. 60606. 1957. 146p.

Film List—Family Relations and Child Development, prepared by Mildred I. Morgan, Nona M. Goodson, and Ruth J. Dales. Rev. ed. Family Relations and Child Development Section, American Home Economics Association, 1600 Twentieth St., N.W., Washington, D.C. 20009. 1960. 31p.

Films about Public Relations and Related Subjects. Information Center, Public Relations Society of America, Inc., 845 Third Ave., New York, N.Y. 10022. 1962. 15p.

Films about the Canning Industry. National Canners Association, 1133 Twentieth St., N.W., Washington, D.C. 20036. 1964. 55p.

Films and Filmstrips on Archaeology. Educational Film Library Association, Inc., 17 W. Sixtieth St., New York, N.Y. 10023. 1958. 11p.

Films, Filmstrips, and Slides on Housing and Community Development:

A Selected Bibliography. Department of Housing and Urban Development Library, 1626 K St., N.W., Washington, D.C. 20410. 1966. 3p. (Superseded by *Urban Outlook: A Selected Bibliography of Films, Filmstrips, Slides, and Audiotapes,* 1969)

Films, Filmstrips, Slides on Worldwide Programs of UNESCO and Agencies with Related Programs. U.S. National Commission for UNESCO, State Department, Washington, D.C. 20025. 1961. 16p.

Films for Action: A Catalogue of Films Dealing with Urban Development and Growth and Related Subjects. Action, Inc., 2 W. Forty-sixth St., New York, N.Y. 10036. 1964. 138p.

Films for Human Relations. Film Division, American Jewish Committee, Institute of Human Relations, 165 E. Fifty-sixth St., New York, N.Y. 10022. 1961. 63p.

Films for Management. Business Screen Magazine, 402 W. Liberty Dr., Wheaton, Ill. 60187. 1961. 17p.

Films for Use in Teaching Theatre. David R. Batcheller, American Educational Theatre Association, 726 Jackson Pl., N.W., Washington, D.C. 20566. 1967. 78p.

Films on North Africa and the Middle East. American Friends of the Middle East, Inc., 1607 New Hampshire, N.W., Washington, D.C. 20009. 1965 with a 1968 revision insert. 46p.

Films on the Handicapped: An Annotated Directory, by Jerome A. Rothstein and Thomas O'Connor. Council for Exceptional Children, National Education Association, 1201 Sixteenth St., N.W., Washington, D.C. 20036. 1955. 56p. Annual supplements, 1957 and 1958.

Films Selected for Use in Discussing Goals for Americans, by Virginia M. Beard, head, Film Bureau of the Cleveland Public Library, 325 Superior Ave., E., Cleveland, Ohio 44114. 1961. 36p.

Filmstrip Guide, edited by Josephine S. Antonini, 3d ed. H. W. Wilson Co., 950 University Ave., New York, N.Y. 10003. 1954. 4-year cumulated supplement, 1955–58. Annual supplements, 1959, 1960, 1961, 1962. Ceased publication in 1962.

Fire Control Film List. Fire Protection Association, 60 Batterymarch St., Boston, Mass. 02110. 1968. 68p.

Free Teaching Materials: Classroom and Curriculum Aids for Elementary School Science, compiled by Roger J. Raimist, Glassboro State College. Conservation and Environmental Science Center for Southern New Jersey, Brown Mills, N.J. 08015. 1969. 57p.

Guide to Federal Safety Films and Film Strips. Federal Safety Council, U.S. Department of Labor, Washington, D.C. 20212. 1963. 43p.

A Guide to Materials Relating to Persons of Mexican Heritage in the U.S. The Mexican-American, A New Focus on Opportunity. Interagency Committee on Mexican-American Affairs, Washington, D.C. 20013.

Guide to Selected Safety Education Films. Rev. ed. National Commission on Safety Education, National Education Association, 1201 Sixteenth St., N.W., Washington, D.C. 20036. 1960. 8p.

Instructional Aids in Industrial Education, by Walter E. Burdette. Division of Industrial Education, Arizona State University, Tempe, Ariz. 85281.

Instructional Materials for Teaching Audiovisual Courses. Audiovisual Center, Syracuse University, in cooperation with the Office of Education, U.S. Department of Health, Education and Welfare, Washington, D.C. 20202. 1961. 74p. (Superseded by *Audiovisual Resources for Teaching Instructional Technology: An Annotated Listing,* 1971)

Instructional Television Materials: A Guide to Films, Kinescopes, and Videotapes Available for Televised Use. 3d ed. National Instructional Television Library Project, 10 Columbus Circle, New York, N.Y. 10019. 1964. 61p.

International Catalog of Mental Health Films. T. L. Pilkington, World Federation for Mental Health, 124 E. Twenty-eighth St., Suite 716, New York, N.Y. 10016. 1960.

The Jazz Record Catalog. M. and N. Harrison, Inc., 274 Madison Ave., New York, N.Y. 10016. Annual.

Libraries and Library Services on Film: A Select List, compiled under the direction of Willard Webb by James H. Culver. U.S. Library of Congress, Reference Department, Washington, D.C. 20541. 2d ed. 1957. 19p.

Marine Science Film Catalog: Movies, Filmstrips, and Slides, by Frank L. Chapman. Carteret County Public Schools, Beaufort, N.C. 28516.

Materials in Russian of Possible Use in High School Classes, by Ilo Remer. Office of Education, U.S. Department of Health, Education and Welfare, Washington, D.C. 20202. 1960. 43p. (Circular no.592, revised)

Materials on Japan: Films, Filmstrips, Records, Paperbacks. Japan Society, Inc., 250 Park Ave., New York, N.Y. 10017. n.d. 29p.

Mental Health Motion Pictures. Publications and Reports Section, Office of the Director, National Institute of Mental Health, Bethesda, Md. 1960. 98p. (Superseded by *Mental Health Film Guide,* 1969)

Motion Picture Films on Planning, Housing and Related Subjects: A Bibliography. American Society of Planning Officials, Chicago, Ill. 1966. 21p.

National Tape Recording Catalog, 1962–63. National Education Association, 1201 Sixteenth St., N.W., Washington, D.C. 20036. 1963. 138p. (Superseded by *National Center for Audio Tapes,* 1970–72)

NEMA Movie Guide to 16mm Films of Electrical Significance, compiled by C. A. Wihtol. National Electrical Manufacturers Association, 155 E. Forty-fourth St., New York, N.Y. 1959. 9p. Supplement, n.d. 3p.

OEO Film Guide, Films for Fighting War on Poverty. Economic Opportunity Office, Executive Office of the President, Washington, D.C. 20506. 1967. 41p.

100 Selected Films in Economic Education. Joint Council on Economic Education, 1212 Avenue of the Americas, New York, N.Y. 10036. 1960. 34p. (Superseded by *Study Materials for Economic Education in the Schools,* 1969)

Program Planner #4—Biography on the 16mm Screen. Educational Film

Library Association, Inc., 17 W. Sixtieth St., New York, N.Y. 10023. 1957. 4p.

Programmed Instruction Materials, 1964–65, compiled and published by The Center for Programed Instruction of the Institute of Educational Technology, Teachers College, Columbia University. Teachers College Press, 525 W. One Hundred and Twentieth St., New York, N.Y. 10027. 1965. 164p.

Selected Films for Migrant Workers. Public Health Service, Division of Community Health Services, U.S. Department of Health, Education and Welfare, Washington, D.C. 20201. 1964. 16p.

Selected Mental Health Films. Mental Health Materials Center, 104 E. Twenty-fifth St., New York, N.Y. 10010. 1967. 119p.

Selected References on Aging: Films on Aging. Administration on Aging, U.S. Department of Health, Education and Welfare, Washington, D.C. 20201. 1965. 43p.

16mm Film Catalog: Popular Level. U.S. Atomic Energy Commission, Washington, D.C. 20545. 1966–67. 75p. (Superseded by *United States Atomic Energy Commission Combined 16mm Film Catalog,* 1970)

16mm Film Catalog: Professional Level. U.S. Atomic Energy Commission, Washington, D.C. 20545. 1966–67. 97p. (Superseded by *United States Atomic Energy Commission Combined 16mm Film Catalog,* 1970)

Spoken Poetry on Records and Tapes: An Index of Currently Available Recordings, compiled by Henry C. Hastings. Association of College and Reference Libraries, American Library Association, 50 E. Huron St., Chicago, Ill. 1957. 51p. (ACRL Monograph no.18)

A Teacher's Handbook of Resources for the Teaching of Health in the Secondary Schools, by Myrtle V. Day. Nebraska State Department of Education, Lincoln, Neb. 68501.

Teacher's Record Catalog, M. and N. Harrison, Inc., 274 Madison Ave., New York, N.Y. 10016. 1960–61. 48p. Annual.

Teaching Aids in the English Language Arts: An Annotated and Critical List, prepared by the Committee on Teaching Aids of the Illinois Association of Teachers of English. National Council of Teachers of English, 508 S. Sixth St., Champaign, Ill. 61820. 1963. 111p.

WRTA: Index. Western Radio and Television Association, 633 Battery St., San Francisco, Calif. 94111. 1967. 22p.

Index

This index covers the four main sections of this publication—(1) catalogs and lists, (2) professional organizations, (3) periodicals, and (4) catalogs and indexes published since 1957 but unavailable in 1971—and the titles, authors, and/or publishers cited in the Preface.

For the main section of this book, Educational Media Catalogs and Lists Generally Available, the Index contains author/publisher, title, and subject references. It also includes type-of-medium references for the single-type-of-medium entries in the main section. It does not include type-of-medium references for the multimedia entries. Index citations to this section of the publication are by entry number not by page; hence they are not preceded by the letter *p*, which in other citations designates page references to all other sections.

For other sections of the publication, citations are to title or name, author and/or publisher, and executive officers as they apply. These citations are page (not entry) references and are distinguished by *p*, which precedes the number and denotes the page references.

ABA Film Guide, 1
Abstract art, *see* Art, Abstract
Accidents—Prevention, 37, 53, 54, 59, 66, 85, 111, 112, 121
Accounting, 91, 96
ACEI Nursery School Education Committee, 63
Ackermann, Jean Marie, 81
Acoustics, 52
ACSSAVO, *see* Association of Chief State School Audio-Visual Officers
Action, Inc., p.92
Addis, Barnett, 68
Addis, Marsha, 68
Administration, *see* Management
Adolescents, 132

Adoption, 132
Adventure and adventurers, 25, 61, 62, 64
Advertising, 51, 109
AECT, *see* Association for Educational Communications and Technology
Aeronautics, 85, 138
Aerospace, *see* Space flight
Africa, 2, 3, 20, 81, 83
African Encounter: A Selected Bibliography of Books, Films, and Other Materials for Promoting an Understanding of Africa among Young Adults, 2
African Film Bibliography 1965, 3
African Heritage and American

History, see The Black Man in Films

Aggression, 24

Agribusiness, *see* Agriculture

Agricultural diseases, 141

Agricultural economics, *see*
Agriculture—Economic aspects

Agricultural engineering, 141

Agricultural pests, 141

Agriculture, 4, 12, 27, 32, 34, 35, 40,
41, 42, 44, 46, 50, 53, 85, 86, 92, 93,
94, 95, 99, 100, 101, 110, 112, 114,
119, 122, 133, 138, 145, 147, 148

Agriculture—Economic aspects, 141

AHIL Quarterly, p.81

Air defense, 87

Air—Pollution, 78

ALA, *see* American Library
Association

Alcoholism, 18, 54, 132

Alexander Graham Bell Association
for the Deaf, Inc., p.90

Allergy, 112

Allison, Mary L., 114

American Academy of Pediatrics,
31, p.91

American art, *see* Art

American Association for Health,
Physical Education, and
Recreation, 136

American Association of Colleges for
Teacher Education, 104

American Association of School
Librarians, p.87

American Bankers Association, 1

American Bar Association, 72

American Council on the Teaching of
Foreign Languages, 77

American Dental Association, 17

American Educational and Historical
Film Center, 5

American Educational Theatre
Association, p.92

American Film Festival Guide, 4, p.78

*American Film Review: Films of
America,* 5

American Foundation on Automation
and Employment, Inc., 71

American Friends of the Middle East,
Inc., p.92

American Geological Institute, p.91

American history, *see* United States—
History

American Home Economics
Association, p.91

*American Indians—An Annotated
Bibliography of Selected Library
Resources,* 6

American Libraries, p.76

American Library Association, p.ix,
2, 64, p.76, p.81, p.82, p.85, p.87,
p.88, p.94

American literature, 11

American Medical Association, 105,
p.91

American Record Guide, p.81

American Science Film Association,
p.81

American Society of Planning
Officials, p.93

American Tape Guide, p.81

Amphetamines, 115

Amphibia, 45

Amputees, 132

Anatomy, 43, 54, 105, 112, 121

Anesthesiology, 105, 112, 121, 134

Animal kingdom, *see* Zoology

Animals—Diseases, *see* Veterinary
medicine

Animals—Habits and behavior, 64, 68

Animated cartoons, 61, 62, 64

*Annotated Bibliography of Audio-
Visual Aids for Management
Development Programs,* p.90

*An Annotated Bibliography of Audio-
visual Materials Related to Understanding and Teaching the
Culturally Disadvantaged,* 7

*Annotated Bibliography of Films in
Automation, Data Processing, and
Computer Science,* 8

*An Annotated Bibliography of
Integrated FLES Teaching
Materials,* 9

*Annotated Bibliography on the
Professional Education of
Teachers,* 10

*Annotated List of Filmstrips for Use
with the Deaf,* p.90

*An Annotated List of Recordings
in the Language Arts,* 11

Antarctic regions, 87

Anthony, Susan B., 28

Anthropological factors in behavior,
68

Anthropology, 27, 91, 110
Antonini, Josephine, p.91, p.92
Apathy, 144
Aphasia, 24
Apprentices, 66
Archaeology, 27
Architecture, 4, 27, 69, 85, 109, 110, 149
Arctic regions, 87
Arizona State University, p.93
Art, 3, 12, 22, 26, 32, 33, 34, 35, 40, 41, 42, 44, 46, 48, 50, 56, 67, 69, 76, 84, 86, 91, 92, 93, 94, 95, 99, 100, 101, 102, 110, 114, 116, 118, 119, 133, 137, 138, 144, 147, 148, *see also* Ceramics; Design; Drawing; Graphic arts; Painting; Sculpture
Art, Abstract, 69
Art education, 137
Art songs, 128
Artificial satellites, 57
Artists, 69
Arts and crafts, 4, 27, 69, 85, 110, 138
ASFA Notes, p.81
Asia, 80, 81
Asia Society, 80
Asian-Americans in the U.S., 47
Association for Childhood Education International, 63
Association for Educational Communications and Technology, p.77, p.79, p.82
Association for Student Teaching, 10
Association of American Railroads, 122
Association of Chief State School Audio-Visual Officers, p.77
Association of Hospital and Institution Libraries, p.81
Astronomy, 12, 32, 34, 35, 38, 40, 41, 42, 44, 50, 86, 91, 92, 93, 94, 95, 99, 100, 101, 110, 114, 119, 133, 139, 147, 148
Atomic energy, 85, 138, 145
Atomic Energy Commission, *see* U.S. Atomic Energy Commission
Attitude (Psychology), 66
Attorneys, *see* Lawyers
Aubrey, Ruth H., 133
Audio, p.81
Audio Cardalog, 12

Audio-Visual Aids for Automation, p.90
Audio-Visual Aids for Counselor Training in Mental Retardation and Emotional Disability, see Catalog of Audio-Visual Aids for Counselor Training in Mental Retardation and Emotional Disability
Audio-Visual Aids for Data Processing Systems, 13
Audio-Visual Aids for International Understanding, p.90
Audiovisual Aids for Teaching Speech in English and Speech Classes of the Secondary School, p.90
Audio-Visual Communications, p.81
Audiovisual education, 18, 19, 58, 121, *see also* Audiovisual equipment; Media production
Audiovisual equipment, 19, 55
Audio-Visual Guidance Materials: An Annotated Bibliography and Directory of Minnesota Sources, 14
An Audio-Visual Guide to Shakespeare, 15
Audiovisual Instruction, p.77, p.82
Audiovisual Market Place, p.viii
Audio-Visual Materials for Teaching about Communism, 16
Audio-Visual Materials for the Teaching of Library Science, see A Working Bibliography of Commercially Available Audio-Visual Materials for the Teaching of Library Science
Audiovisual Materials in Dentistry, 17
Audio-Visual Media and Materials on Mental Retardation, p.90
Audio-Visual Resource Guide, 18
Audiovisual Resources for Grades K–8, p.viii
Audiovisual Resources for Teaching Instructional Technology: An Annotated Listing, 19
Autism, 24
Auto mechanics, 138
Auto theft, 118
Automation and data processing, 1, 8, 13, 79, 85, 145
Automobiles, 85
Autopsy, 112
AV Communication Review, p.77, p.82

AVCR, see AV Communication Review
AVI, see Audiovisual Instruction
Aviation, *see* Aeronautics
Awareness, 144

Baby sitters, 31, 132
Ballads, 75
Ballet, 126
Band, 52, 65
Banks and banking, 1, 96, 138
Bar, *see* Lawyers
Batcheller, David R., p.92
Beard, Virginia M., p.92
Beasts, *see* Animal—Habits and
   behavior
Beef cattle, *see* Cattle
Behavior, 68
Behavioral sciences, 120
Belief, 144
Bell, Violet M., **80**
Benschoter, Reba A., 43
Bible, 18, 140
Bibliography of Audio-Visual Aids for
   Courses in American Literature, p.90
Bibliography of Films on Aerospace
   Medicine, p.90
Bicycles and bicycling, 31
Bildersee, Max U., 12
Bill of Rights, *see* U.S. Constitution—
   Amendments
Billboard Publications, Inc., p.84
Biographies, 52
Biographies for Junior High: A List
   of Biographies and Correlated
   Audiovisual Aids, p.90
Biography, 3, 15, 18, 21, 25, 72, 82, 88
Biology, 12, 32, 34, 35, 38, 40, 41, 42,
   44, 46, 50, 54, 73, 86, 91, 92, 93, 94,
   95, 99, 100, 101, 110, 112, 114, 119,
   121, 133, 138, 145, 146, 147, 148
Biology, Marine, *see* Marine biology
Birds, 138
The Black Man in Films—African
   Heritage and American History, 20
The Black Record: A Selective
   Discography of Afro-America on
   Audio Discs, 21
Blind, 132
Blue Book of Audiovisual Materials, 22
Boating Films Directory, 23
Boats and boating, 23
Body, 121, 144

Bookkeeping, 96, 150
The Booklist, p.76, p.82
Books for children, *see* Children's
   literature
Books on Magnetic Tape: A Catalog
   of Tape Recordings Which
   Supplement the Talking Book
   Program, p.91
Botany, 12, 32, 34, 35, 38, 40, 41, 42,
   44, 45, 46, 50, 86, 92, 93, 94, 95, **99**,
   100, 101, 114, 119, 133, 147, 148
R. R. Bowker Co., p.viii, p.ix, 92, 93,
   94, 95, p.88
Bray, Mayfield, p.viii
Brian, Sister Mary, p.90
Bristow, Allen P., 117
Bro-Dart Foundation, p.ix, 44
Bruyn, Henry B., 115
Budgets, Household, 1, 130
Building, 85, 109
Burdette, Walter E., p.93
Bureau of Education for the
   Handicapped, 25
Business, 1, 5, 12, 25, 26, 27, 32, **33**,
   34, 35, 40, 41, 42, 44, 46, 50, 85,
   86, 91, 92, 93, 94, 95, 96, 99, **100**,
   101, 110, 114, 119, 133, 138, 147,
   148, 150
Business Screen, p.82
Business Screen Magazine, p.91, **p.92**

Cain, Robert, 76
Calligraphy, *see* Writing
Camp songs, 123
Cancer, 43, 54, 112, 131, 134, 152
Cancer Film Guide, 1963, p.91
Captioned Films for the Deaf, see
   Catalog of Captioned Films
   for the Deaf
Cardiovascular system, 112
Careers, *see* Vocational guidance
Carmichael, Stokely, 83
Carpenter, Anita A., 25
Carpentry, 85
Carr, William G., 27
Carteret County (N.C.) Public Schools,
   p.93
Cartography, *see* Maps
Catalog of Audio-Visual Aids for
   Counselor Training in Mental
   Retardation and Emotional
   Disability, Vol. 1: Films, 24

Catalog of Captioned Films for the Deaf, 25
A Catalog of Folk Songs, Ballads, Dances, Instrumental Pieces, and Folk Tales of the United States and Latin America on Phonograph Records, see *Folk Music*
Catalog of Recorded Instruction for Television, 26
Catalog of Selected Films on Pediatrics and Child Health, p.91
Cattle, 141
Ceramics, see Pottery
Cerebral palsy, 113, 132
Chapman, Frank L., p.93
Chemicals, Chemistry, and Chemical Industry, see *Film Guide on Chemicals, Chemistry and Chemical Industry*
Chemistry, 12, 32, 34, 35, 38, 40, 41, 42, 44, 46, 50, 53, 54, 73, 86, 91, 92, 93, 94, 95, 99, 100, 101, 110, 112, 114, 119, 133, 146, 147, 148
Child development, see Children— Care and hygiene
Child study, 48, 63, 132
Children—Care and hygiene, 54, 63, 113, 121, 132
Children—Nutrition, 130
Children's literature, 22, 61, 89, 140, see also Fables; Fairy tales; Legends
Children's Record Reviews, p.91
Children's Services Division, p.76, p.88
China—Communism, see Communism—China
Chinese language, 91
Choice, p.76
Choice Reviews-on-Cards, p.76
Christmas music, 123
Church work, 18
Cigarettes, 152
CINE/70 Golden Eagle Film Awards, 27
Cinema, see Films
Citation Press, 114
Citizenship, 72, 103, 116
City, 144
City planning, 70
Civics, see Citizenship; Political science
Civil defense, 54, 105, 112, 117

Civil rights, 18, 28, 72, 83, 103
Civil Rights: A Selected List of Films, Filmstrips, and Recordings, 28
The Civil War in Motion Pictures, A Bibliography of Films Produced in the United States since 1897, 29
Claremont House, 97
Classical languages, see Latin language
Classical music, 89, 123, 126
Clift, David H., p.76
Clinical medicine, 43
Clothing, 125
Clugston, Katharine W., 148
Collective bargaining, 66
College and Research Libraries, p.77
College Film Library Collection, p.ix
Collier, Richard E., 10
Colonialism, 3
Columbia University, 130, p.94
Comic opera, see Opera
Commercial banking, 1
Committee of Food and Nutrition Films and Filmstrips, 130
Communication, 19, 26, 48, 85, 91, **98**, 109, 121, 144
Communism, 5, 16, 39, 72, 117
Communism—China, 16, 74
Communism—Cuba, 74
Communism—Germany, 16
Communism—Russia, 16, 74
Communism—United States, 16, 74
Community life, 103, 130, 144
Community service, 24
Composite List of Conservation and Related Film Titles, p.91
Comprehensive Service Corp., 42
Computer Assisted Instruction, see *Index to Computer Assisted Instruction*
Computer-Assisted Instruction Guide, p.91
Computer control, see Automation and data processing
Computers, 91, see also Technology
Computers, Electronic, see Electronic computers
Conservation, 88, 138
Conservation and Environmental Science Center for Southern New Jersey, p.92
Conservation League, p.91

Conservation of Forests, *see*
  Natural resources
Conservation of the soil, *see* Soil
  conservation
Conservation of wildlife, *see*
  Wildlife—Conservation
Constellations, *see* Astronomy
Constitution, *see* U.S. Constitution
Constitutional amendments—U.S.,
  see U.S. Constitution—
  Amendments
Construction, *see* Architecture;
  Building; Engineering
Consumer education, 51, 96
Contemporary music, 123
Cook, James A., 74
Cookery, 85
Corn, 141
Coronary heart diseases, *see*
  Heart—Diseases
Cory, Patricia Blair, p.90
Council for Exceptional Children, p.92
Council of Planning Librarians, 70, 143
Council on International Nontheatrical
  Events, 27
Counseling, 14, 22, 24, 25, 36, 48, 87,
  91, 130, 144, 150
Courts, 72
Crafts, *see* Arts and crafts
Creativeness, 85
Credit, 1
*A Critical Index of Films and Filmstrips
  in Conservation Dealing with
  Renewable Resources, Non-
  Renewable Resources, Resources
  and People, and Ecology,* p.91
Culturally deprived, *see* Socially
  handicapped
Cultures, 84, 103
Culver, James H., p.93
Customs, 84
Cuttill, William, p.83
Cytology, 45, 112

Dairying, 141
Dales, Ruth J., p.91
Dalglish, William A., 103
Dance, 110, 123
Dance music, 75
Data Education Films, see *Guide to
  Data Education Films*
Data processing, *see* Automation and
  data processing
Data Processing Management
  Association, 13
Dating (Social customs), 103
Day, Myrtle V., p.94
Deaf—Means of communicating, 132
Decorative arts, *see* Arts and crafts
Delinquency, Juvenile, *see* Juvenile
  delinquency
Democracy, 87
Dental health, 17
Dentistry, 17, 54, 112, 121
Department of Housing and Urban
  Development Library, p.92
Depressants, 115
Dermatology, 43, 105
Design, 56, 69, 110
*Development and Structure of Industry
  —Instructional Aids List and
  Bibliography,* 30
Dever, Esther, 138
Devereux Foundation Institute for
  Research and Training, 24
Dick, Esmé, p.78
Diffor, John W., 34, 35
Dimitroff, Lillian, 7
*A Directory of 8mm and 16mm Sound
  Feature Films Available for Rental
  in the United States,* see *Feature
  Films on 8 and 16*
Directory of Geoscience Films, p.91
A Directory of Safety Films, 31
*Directory of Summer Session Courses
  on Educational Media,* p.78
Disarmament, 74
Discipline, *see* Mental discipline
Discrimination, 28, 83, 144
Diseases, 37, 113
Diseases and pests, *see* Agricultural
  pests; Plant diseases
Distributive education, 96, 150
Dodge, James W., p.79
Drafting, Mechanical, 69
Drama, 11, 15, 76, 110, 140
Dramatic music, *see* Opera
Drawing, 56, 69
Driver education, 25, 26
Drug education, 26
Drug habit, *see* Narcotic habit
Drugs, 24, 43, 54, 85, 87, 105, 112,
  115, 121, 129
Du Kane Corporation, 33

Ear, 54, 113, 121
Early childhood education, *see*
  Child study
Earth sciences, 12, 22, 32, 34, 35, 38,
  40, 41, 42, 44, 46, 50, 86, 92, 93,
  94, 95, 99, 100, 101, 114, 119,
  133, 147, 148
Eastern Baptist College, 5
Eastman Kodak Co., 55
Economic Opportunity Office, p.93
Economics, 1, 4, 12, 25, 32, 33, 34, 35,
  40, 41, 42, 44, 46, 48, 50, 66, 83,
  86, 88, 91, 92, 93, 94, 95, 96, 99,
  100, 101, 110, 114, 119, 133, **138**,
  142, 147, 148, 150
ect, p.77
Education, 12, 18, 19, 22, 26, 27, 28,
  32, 34, 35, 40, 41, 42, 43, 44, 46,
  50, 70, 86, 91, 92, 93, 94, 95, 99,
  100, 101, 102, 103, 110, 114, 119,
  133, 147, 148
Education—Culturally deprived, 7
Education—Research, 19
Education—Study and teaching, 18
Education, Higher, 90
Education, Physical, *see* Physical
  education and training
Education, Vocational, *see* Vocational
  education
Educational associations, 90
Educational Broadcasting Institute,
  p.79
Educational Broadcasting Review,
  p. 79, p.83
Educational facilities, 19
Educational Film Guide, p.91
Educational Film Library Association,
  Inc., 4, 15, 16, 28, 41, 42, 49, 50,
  57, 58, 61, 66, 67, 115, 151, p.78,
  p.88, p.91, pp.93–94
Educational films, *see* Motion pictures
  in education
Educational guidance, *see* Personnel
  service in education
Educational Information Collection,
  p.viii
Educational Information Services, Inc.,
  p.viii
Educational Media, p.83
Educational Media Council, Inc.,
  32, p.78
Educational Media in Programs for the

Culturally Disadvantaged and
  Vocational Education, p.78
Educational Media Index, p.78
Educational Media Index: A Project
  of the Educational Media
  Council, 32
Educational Media Project, 3
Educational Product Report, p.83
Educational Products Information
  Exchange Institute, p.83
Educational Screen and Audiovisual
  Guide, 22
Educational Screen AV Guide, p.83
Educational Sound Filmstrip
  Directory, 33
Educational Technology, p.84
Educational Television, p.84
Educators Guide to Free Films, 34
Educators Guide to Free Filmstrips, 35
Educators Guide to Free Guidance
  Materials, 36
Educators Guide to Free Health,
  Physical Education and Recreation
  Materials, 37
Educators Guide to Free
  Science Materials, 38
Educators Guide to Free Slidefilms,
  see *Educators Guide to Free*
  Filmstrips
Educators Guide to Free Social
  Studies Materials, 39
Educators Guide to Free Tapes,
  Scripts, and Transcriptions, 40
Educator's Guide to Media and
  Methods, see *Media & Methods*
Educators Progress Service, 34, 35,
  36, 37, 38, 39, 40
Educators Purchasing Master—
  Audiovisual, p.viii
J. W. Edwards, Inc., 101, 102
EFLA, *see* Educational Film Library
  Association, Inc.
EFLA Bulletin, p.88
EFLA Evaluations, 41
8mm Cartridges, see *Index to 8mm*
  Motion Cartridges
8mm Film Directory, 42
8mm Films in Medicine and Health
  Sciences, 43
Electricity, 138
Electronic computers, 8
Electronic music, 126

*The Elementary School Library
Collection: A Guide to Books and
Other Media,* 44
Embalming, 112
Embryology, 43, 105, 112
EMC, *see* Educational Media Council
Employer-employee relations, *see*
Industrial relations
Employment, 28
*The Encyclopaedia Cinematographica
—English Translation of Film Titles
Listed in 1967 Index,* 45
Endodontia, 134
Engineering, 12, 32, 34, 35, 40, 41, 42,
44, 46, 48, 50, 73, 86, 91, 92, 93,
94, 95, 99, 100, 101, 110, 114, 119,
133, 145, 147, 148
English language, 33, 91, 140, 144
English poetry, 11
Enoch Pratt Free Library, 20
*Entelek CAI/CMI Information
Exchange,* 46
Entelek Incorporated, 46, 118, p.91
Environmental health, 54, 70, 78, 112,
121, 151
Epilepsy, 24, 113
ERIC Clearinghouse on Educational
Media and Technology, 47, p.87
Espionage, 74
*Ethnic Studies and Audiovisual Media:
A Listing and Discussion,* 47
Ethnology, 47
Evaluation techniques, 24
Evangelistic work, 3
Evolution, 112
Eye, 54, 112, 113, 121

Fables, 61, 62, 64
Fact Book, 48
Fairy tales, 61, 62, 64, 123
Faith, 103
Family, 18, 103
Family budget, *see* Budgets,
Household
Family life education, 14, 132
*Farm Film Guide, 1965–1966:
A Comprehensive Listing of Films
and Filmstrips Relating to All
Phases of Agribusiness,* p.91
Farm mechanics, *see* Agricultural
engineering
Farming, *see* Agriculture

Farms, 31, 111
Farwell, Gail F., 36
Fauna, *see* Animals—Habits and
behavior; Zoology
Fearon Publishers, 133
*Feature Films on 8 and 16:
A Directory of 8mm and 16mm
Sound Feature Films Available
for Rental in the United States,* 49
Federal Safety Council, p.92
Ferguson, Ralph, p.77
Fiks, A. I., 77
Film Bureau of the Cleveland Public
Library, p.92
Film Evaluation Guide, 1946–64, 50
Film Guide for Industrial Training, p.91
*Film Guide for Marketing
Executives,* 51
Film Guide for Music Educators, 52
*Film Guide on Chemicals, Chemistry
and the Chemical Industry,* 53
Film Library Information Council,
p.78, p.84
Film Library Quarterly, p.79, p.84
*Film List—Family Relations and Child
Development,* p.91
Film News Co., p.84
*Film News: The International Review
of AV Materials and
Equipment,* p.84
*Film Reference Guide for Medicine
and Allied Sciences,* 54
Film Sense, 81
*A Filmography of Films about Movies
and Movie Making,* 55
Films, 34, 41, 42, 49, 50, 55, 92, 94,
99, 101
*Films about Public Relations and
Related Subjects,* p.91
Films about the Canning Industry, p.91
*Films Adaptable to the Teaching of
Nursing Subjects,* see *A Quick
Reference List of Recent Films
Adaptable to the Teaching of
Nursing Subjects*
*Films and Filmstrips for Art
Education K–12,* 56
*Films and Filmstrips for the Space
Age,* 57
Films and Filmstrips on Archaeology,
p.91
Films and Filmstrips on Audio-Visual

Materials and Methods, 58

Films and Filmstrips on Forestry, 59

Films and Librarians: A Selected List of 16mm Films Useful in the Field of Librarianship, 60

Films, Filmstrips, and Slides on Housing and Community Development: A Selected Bibliography, p.91

Films, Filmstrips, Maps and Globes, Records on Asia, see A Guide to Films, Filmstrips, Maps and Globes, Records on Asia

Films, Filmstrips, Slides on Worldwide Programs of UNESCO and Agencies with Related Programs, p.92

Films for Action: A Catalogue of Films Dealing with Urban Development and Growth and Related Subjects, p.92

Films for Children, 61

Films for Children: A Selected List, 62

Films for Early Childhood Education, 63

Films for Human Relations, p.92

Films for Libraries, 64

Films for Management, p.92

Films for Music Education and Opera Films: An International Selective Catalogue, 65

Films for Personnel Management: An Annotated Directory of 16mm Films, Filmstrips, and Videotapes, 66

Films for Use in Teaching Theatre, p.92

Films for Young Adults: A Selected List, 67

Films in Automation, Data Processing, and Computer Science, see Annotated Bibliography of Films in Automation, Data Processing, and Computer Science

Films in the Behavioral Sciences: An Annotated Catalogue, 68

Films of America, see American Film Review

Films on Art, 69

Films on Community Affairs: Urban and Rural, 70

Films on International Development, see Guide to Films on International Development

Films on Jobs, Training and the Ghetto: An Evaluative Guide, 71

Films on Legal Subjects for Bar and Public Showings: A Listing of the Films and Sources, 72

Films on North Africa and the Middle East, p.92

Films on Oceanography, 73

Films on the Handicapped: An Annotated Directory, p.92

Films Relating to Communism, 74

Films Selected for Use in Discussing Goals for Americans, p.92

Films (16mm) about Famous People, see Guide to Films (16mm) about Famous People

Films (16mm) about Negroes, see Guide to Films (16mm) about Negroes

Filmstrip Guide, p.92

Filmstrips, 33, 35, 95, 101

Finance, 96, 109, 138

Financial planning, 1

Fine arts, see Art; Music

Fire Control Film List, p.92

Fire prevention, 31, 85, 88

Fire Protection Association, p.92

Firearms, 31

First aid in illness and injury, 31, 37, 43, 54, 105, 112, 117, 121

Fish, 88

Fisher Publishing Inc., p.viii

Fishing, 85, 88

FLES Teaching Materials, see An Annotated Bibliography of Integrated FLES Teaching Materials

FLIC, see Film Library Information Council

Flory, Elizabeth, 41

Folk music, 89, 123, 126

Folk Music: A Catalog of Folk Songs, Ballads, Dances, Instrumental Pieces, and Folk Tales of the United States and Latin America on Phonograph Records, 75

Folk songs, 21, 75

Folklore, 11

Food, 37, 85, 130

Food and Nutrition Council of Greater New York, Inc., 130

Ford Film Collection in the National Archives, p.viii

Foreign Government Loan Films (16mm) in the United States, see *Guide to Foreign-Government Loan Films (16mm) in the United States*

Foreign Language Audio-Visual Guide, 76

Foreign Language Programmed Materials: 1969, 77

Foreign languages, see individual language; Languages, Modern; Latin language

Forest fires, 59

Forests, 85

Forests and forestry, 4, 59, 138, 141

Forgery, 117

4-H Clubs, 141

Free Films, see *Educators Guide to Free Films*

Free Films on Air Pollution, 78

Free Filmstrips, see *Educators Guide to Free Filmstrips*

Free Guidance Materials, see *Educators Guide to Free Guidance Materials*

Free Health, Physical Education and Recreation Materials, see *Educators Guide to Free Health, Physical Education and Recreation Materials*

Free-Loan Training Films (16mm), see *Guide to Free-Loan Training Films (16mm)*

Free Science Materials, see *Educators Guide to Free Science Materials*

Free Social Studies Materials, see *Educators Guide to Free Social Studies Materials*

Free Tapes, Scripts, and Transcriptions, see *Educators Guide to Free Tapes, Scripts, and Transcriptions*

Free Teaching Materials: Classroom and Curriculum Aids for Elementary School Science, p.92

Freedom, 144

French language, 9, 77, 91, 108, 124

Friedlander, Madeline S., 151

Friendship, 144

Friese, Eugene, p.viii

Fruit, 141

Fruit culture, 141

Fuels, 145

Future Farmers of America, 141

Gages, 85

Gangs, see Juvenile delinquency

Gardening, 130

Garvey, Marcus, 83

Gas, 85, 138

Gaver, Mary V., 44

General interest, 146

General science, 146

Generation gap, 144

Genetics, 105, 112

Geography, 4, 12, 22, 26, 32, 34, 35, 39, 40, 41, 42, 44, 46, 50, 76, 86, 91, 92, 93, 94, 95, 99, 100, 101, 102, 110, 114, 118, 119, 133, 147, 148

Geology, 73, 91, 110

German language, 9, 77, 91, 108, 124

Germany—Communism, see Communism—Germany

Gerontology, 112, 121

Ghetto life, 83

God, 18, 103

Goodman, Louis S., and Associates, 66

Goodson, Nona M., p.91

Government, see Political science

Government-Loan Film (16mm), see *Guide to Government-Loan Film (16mm)*

Grand opera, see Opera

Graphic arts, 56, 110

Great Plains National Instructional Television Library, 26, p.86

Greene, Ellin, p.viii

Greenhill, Leslie P., 45

Greer, Sara, 98

Grooming, Personal, 36

Grubbs, Eloyse, 148

Guidance, see Counseling; Personnel service in education; Vocational guidance

Guide to Data Education Films, 79

Guide to Federal Safety Films and Film Strips, p.92

A Guide to Films, Filmstrips, Maps and Globes, Records on Asia, 80

Guide to Films on International Development, 81

*Guide to Films (16mm) about
Famous People,* 82
*Guide to Films (16mm)
about Negroes,* 83
*Guide to Foreign-Government Loan
Film (16mm) in the
United States,* 84
*Guide to Free-Loan Training Films
(16mm),* 85
*Guide to Government-Loan Film
(16mm),* 86
*A Guide to Materials Relating to
Persons of Mexican Heritage in
the U.S. The Mexican-American,
A New Focus on Opportunity,* p.92
*Guide to Military-Loan Film
(16mm),* 87
*Guide to Selected Safety Education
Films,* p.92
Guide to State-Loan Film (16mm), 88
Guided missiles, 57, 87
*Guidelines for Audiovisual Materials
and Services for Public
Libraries,* p.76
Guides to Newer Educational Media,
p.vii
Guns, *see* Firearms
Guss, Carolyn, p.83, p.88
Gynecology, 105

Hallucinogens, 115
Handicapped, *see* Mentally
handicapped; Physically
handicapped
Handicrafts, 69
Harbrace Publications, Inc., p.82
Harley, William G., p.79
Harmon, John T., 108
M. & N. Harrison, Inc., 89, p.93, p.94
*Harrison Tape Catalog: 8-Track,
Cassettes, Open-Reel,* 89
Hartley, William H., 39
Hastings, Henry C., p.94
Hawaiian music, 89
Health, *see* Hygiene
Health, Dental, *see* Dental health
Health education, 22, 91, 105
Health, Mental, *see* Mental health
Health, Physical, *see* Physical health
Health, Public, *see* Public health
Heart—Diseases, 54, 131, 152
Hebrew language, 124

Hendershot, Carl, 119
Henry Ford Centennial Library, 135
Hereditary factors in behavior, 68
Heredity, 112
Heroin, 115
High Fidelity, p.84
Highways, 88
History, 4, 5, 12, 22, 26, 27, 32, 34, 35,
39, 40, 41, 42, 44, 46, 50, 57, 58,
72, 76, 84, 86, 88, 91, 92, 93, 94,
95, 99, 100, 101, 102, 110, 114, 118,
119, 122, 133, 144, 147, 148
Hitchens, Howard B., Jr., p.77
Hobbies, 64
Hockman, William S., p.84
Holidays, 61, 62, 64
Home and school, 63
Home economics, 12, 32, 34, 35, 40,
41, 42, 44, 46, 50, 53, 85, 86, 91,
92, 93, 94, 95, 99, 100, 101, 110,
114, 119, 133, 138, 141, 147, 148
Home furnishings, 125
Home life, *see* Family
Hopkinson, Shirley L., 97
Horkheimer, Foley A., 37
Horkheimer, Mary Foley, 34, 35
Horticulture, *see* Gardening
Horvat, John J., 90
Hospitals, 24, 43, 105, 112, 121
Housing, 18, 70, 109, 111, 149
Human body, *see* Physiology
Human race, *see* Anthropology
Human relations, 22, 39, 66, 112, 144
Human rights, *see* Civil rights
Humanities, 26, 48
Humor, *see* Wit and humor
Humphreys, Alfred W., 69
Hunting, 88
Hydraulics, 85
Hygiene, 12, 32, 34, 35, 37, 40, 41, 42,
44, 46, 48, 50, 53, 70, 86, 92, 93, 94,
95, 99, 100, 101, 103, 112, 114, 119,
121, 133, 138, 144, 147, 148
Hygiene—Study and teaching, *see*
Health education
Hypnosis, 24

*An Index of Media for Use in
Instruction in Educational
Administration,* 90
*Index to Computer Assisted
Instruction,* 91

Index to 8mm Motion Cartridges, 92
Index to Overhead Transparencies, 93
Index to 16mm Educational Films, 94
*Index to 35mm Educational
    Filmstrips,* 95
Indiana Department of Commerce, 70
Indiana Language Program, 9
Indiana University, p.vii, p.ix, 3, 9, p.87
Indiana University School of
    Nursing, 121
Indians, American, 6
Industrial arts, 138
Industrial arts education, 69
Industrial engineering, *see*
    Industrial management
Industrial management, 30, **96**
Industrial relations, 66
Industry, 1, 27, 30, 76, 111, 130
Information Coordinators, Inc., 128
Insects, Injurious and beneficial, 59
Institute of Human Relations, p.92
Institute of Traffic Engineers, 127
*Instructional Aids in Industrial
    Education,* p.93
Instructional design, 19
*Instructional Materials for Adult
    Business and Distributive
    Education,* 96
*Instructional Materials for Teaching
    Audiovisual Courses,* p.93
*Instructional Materials for Teaching
    the Use of the Library,* 97
Instructional techniques, 19
*Instructional Television Materials:
    A Guide to Films, Kinescopes, and
    Videotapes Available for
    Televised Use,* p.93
Instrumental music, 65, 75
Insurance, 66, 96, 109, *see also*
    Social security
Integration, Racial, *see* Race problems
Interagency Committee on
    Mexican-American Affairs, **p.92**
Interior decoration, 69
International affairs, 72
*International Catalog of Mental
    Health Films,* p.93
International economics, 142
International Music Centre, Vienna, 65
International relations, 18, 39, 84, 87,
    91
Interviewing, 66

Invertebrates, 45
Investment banking, 1
Italian language, 108, 124

Japan Society, Inc., p.93
Japanese language, 91
Jazz music, 65, 89, 126
The Jazz Record Catalog, p.93
*JEA Media Guide: A National Guide
    to the Choice of Audiovisual Titles
    for Use in the Study of Modern
    Communications,* 98
Jewelry, 69
Job analysis, 66, 71
Johnson, Harry, p.ix
Joint Council on Economic
    Education, 142, p.93
JOLA Technical Communications, p.77
Jones, Emily S., p.ix, 41, 42
Journal of Library Automation, p.77
Journal of the SMPTE, p.85
*Journal of the University Film
    Association,* p.80, p.85
Journalism, 12, 26, 32, 34, 35, 40, 41,
    42, 44, 46, 50, 86, 92, 93, 94, 95,
    99, 100, 101, 102, 114, 119,
    133, 147, 148
Journalism Education Association, 98
Justice, 103
Juvenile delinquency, 24, 72, 132
Juvenile literature, *see* Children's
    literature

Keesee, Elizabeth, 124
Kinescopes and videotapes, 26, 48
King, Martin Luther, Jr., 83
Kishankee College, 98
Kitterman, Carolyn H., 70
Klain, Ambrose, 143
Kone, Grace Ann, 42
Kuhns, William, 144

Labor relations, *see* Industrial
    relations
Landers, Bertha, 76
Landers Associates, 76, 99
Landers Film Reviews, 99
Language and languages, 12, 22, 26,
    32, 34, 35, 40, 41, 42, 44, 46, 50, **67**,
    76, 77, 86, 89, 92, 93, 94, 95, 99,
    100, 101, 102, 108, 114, 118, 119,
    123, 133, 144, 147, 148

Language arts, *see* Communication;
   English language; Literature;
   Reading; Speech
Languages, Modern, 9, 25, 26, 48
Lanier, Vincent, 137
Larson, L. C., p.83
Latchaw, Truly Trousdale, 14
Latin America, 81
Latin language, 48, 77, 91
Law, 72, 96
Lawyers, 72, 118
Layer, Harold A., 47
Leadership, 5, 66, 144
Learning, Psychology of, 24, 68
Learning Directory 1970–71, 100
Legal medicine, *see* Medical
   jurisprudence
Legal profession, *see* Lawyers
Legends, 61, 62, 64
Levison, Melvin E., 80
Librarianship, *see* Library science
*Libraries and Library Services on
   Film: A Select List,* p.93
Library of Congress, 29, 101, 102
*Library of Congress Catalog: Motion
   Pictures and Filmstrips,* 101
*Library of Congress Catalog: Music
   and Phonorecords,* 102
*Library Resources and Technical
   Services,* p.77
Library science, 12, 32, 34, 35, 40,
   41, 42, 44, 46, 50, 60, 86, 91, 92,
   93, 94, 95, 97, 99, 100, 101, 114,
   119, 133, 147, 148, 153
Library Technology Program, p.76, p.85
Library Technology Reports, p.76,
   p.85
Lieberman, Irving, 153
Likan, Helen A., 91
Limbacher, James L., 49, 135
Linguistics, *see* Language and
   languages
Literature, 5, 12, 22, 25, 32, 34, 35,
   40, 41, 42, 44, 46, 50, 76, 84, 86,
   92, 93, 94, 95, 99, 100, 101, 102,
   114, 118, 119, 133, 147, 148
Lithography, 69
Logging, *see* Lumber and lumbering
Los Angeles County Schools, 116
Lovan, Nora Geraldine, 8
Love, 103
Luce, Arnold, 14

Lumber and lumbering, 59
Lundgaard, Harriet, p.78

Macauley, C. Cameron, 115
McGraw-Hill Book Co., 32
McIntyre, Kenneth M., 139
Malnutrition, *see* Nutrition
Mammals, 45
Management, 19, 51, 66, 91, 112
Manual on Film Evaluation, p.78
Manual training, *see* Industrial
   arts education
Manufacturing Chemists' Association,
   Inc., 53
Maps, 39, 59, 85
Marijuana, 115
Marine biology, 27
*Marine Science Film Catalog: Movies,
   Filmstrips, and Slides,* p.93
Marketing Executives, see *Film Guide
   for Marketing Executives*
Markets, 142
Marquis, Chalmers, p.79
Marriage, 103
Mass communication, *see*
   Communication
*Materials in Russian of Possible Use
   in High School Classes,* p.93
*Materials on Japan: Films, Filmstrips,
   Records, Paperbacks,* p.93
Maternal welfare, *see* Mothers
Mathematics, 4, 12, 22, 26, 32, 33, 34,
   35, 40, 41, 42, 44, 46, 48, 50, 86,
   91, 92, 93, 94, 95, 99, 100, 101, 110,
   114, 119, 133, 138, 144, 147, 148
Maurice Falk Medical Fund, 115
Meal planning, *see* Nutrition
Measurement, 85
Mechanical drafting, *see* Drafting,
   Mechanical
Media & Methods, p.86
Media & Methods Institute, Inc., p.86
Media for Christian Formation, 103
*Media for Use in Instruction in
   Educational Administration,* see
   *An Index of Media for Use in
   Instruction in Educational
   Administration*
Media production, 55, 58
*Mediated Teacher Education
   Resources,* 104
Medical and Surgical Motion Pictures:

A Catalog of Selected Films, 105
Medical jurisprudence, 105
Medical profession, *see* Medicine
Medical technology, 105
Medicine, 12, 27, 32, 34, 35, 40, 41,
    42, 44, 46, 50, 68, 72, 86, 92, 93,
    94, 95, 99, 100, 101, 102, 105, 110,
    112, 113, 114, 119, 121, 133,
    145, 147, 148
Medicine and Allied Sciences, see
    *Film Reference Guide for Medicine
    and Allied Sciences*
Medicine, Veterinary, *see* Veterinary
    medicine
Meetings, Public, *see* Public meetings
Meierhenry, W. C., 104
Memoirs, *see* Biography
Mental discipline, 66
Mental health, 18, 24, 106
Mental Health Film Guide, 106
Mental Health Materials Center, p.94
Mental Health Motion Pictures, p.93
Mental hygiene, *see* Mental health
Mental retardation, 24, 107, 113
Mental Retardation Film List, 107
Mentally handicapped, 132
Merchandising, 51
Metals, 85
Meteorology, 110, 139
Mexicans in the U.S., 47
Meyer Library Audio Catalog, p.viii
Meyers, Arthur S., 20
Microbiology, 45, 54, 112, 121
Middle East, *see* Asia
Military art and science, 110
*Military-Loan Film (16mm), see Guide
    to Military-Loan Film (16mm)*
Miller, Helen B., 9
Minerals, 85
Mining, 85
Mining engineering, 145
Minnesota State Department of
    Education, 14
Missiles, Guided, *see* Guided missiles
*MLA Selective List of Materials for
    Use by Teachers of Modern Foreign
    Languages in Elementary and
    Secondary Schools,* 108
Modern Language, *see* Languages,
    Modern
Modern Language Association of
    America, 77, 108

Modern Media Teacher, p.86
Money, 1
Morale, 66
Morals, *see* Behavior
Morgan, Mildred I., p.91
Morphine, 115
Mosaics, 69
Mothers, 54, 112
*Motion Picture Films on Planning,
    Housing and Related Subjects:
    A Bibliography,* p.93
Motion pictures, *see* Films
Motion pictures, Documentary, 22, 55
Motion Pictures and Filmstrips, see
    *Library of Congress Catalog:
    Motion Pictures and Filmstrips*
Motion Pictures and Slide Films, 109
Motion pictures in education, 22, 58
Motivation (Psychology), 66
Mountz, Louise Smith, p.90
*Movies for a Course in Urban
    Planning, see Suggested Series of
    Movies for a Course in Urban
    Planning*
Moving pictures, *see* Films
*A Multi-Media Approach to Children's
    Literature,* p.viii
*Multimedia Materials for
    Afro-American Studies,* p.ix
Murals, 69
Museums, 69
Music, 3, 12, 22, 32, 33, 34, 35, 40, 41,
    42, 44, 46, 50, 65, 76, 84, 86, 89, 91,
    92, 93, 94, 95, 99, 100, 101, 102,
    110, 114, 119, 123, 126, 133,
    135, 138, 147, 148, *see also*
    Band; Orchestra
Music—Study and teaching, 65
Music and Phonorecords, see *Library
    of Congress Catalog: Music and
    Phonorecords*
Music Educators National
    Conference, 52
Music festivals, 65
Music Library Association, p.86
Musical instruments, 65
Musicians, 65

NAEB, *see* National Association of
    Educational Broadcasters
NAEB Newsletter, p.79
NALLD, *see* National Association of

Language Laboratory Directors
NALLD Journal, p. 79, p.86
Narcotic habit, 18, 121, 129
Narcotics, 117
National Aeronautics and Space
  Administration, 139
National Air Pollution
  Administration, 78
National Archives and Records
  Service, 147
National Art Education Association,
  69, 137
National Association for Retarded
  Children, p.90
National Association of Educational
  Broadcasters, p.77, p.79, p.83
National Association of Engine and
  Boat Manufacturers, 23
National Association of Language
  Laboratory Directors, p.79, p.86
National Association of Real Estate
  Boards, 109
National Canners Association, p.91
National Center for Audio Tapes, 110
*National Center for Audio Tapes
  Catalog, 1970–72,* 110
National Clearinghouse for Drug
  Abuse Information, 129
National Clearinghouse for Smoking
  and Health, 152
National Commission on Safety
  Education, p.92
National Council of Teachers of
  English, 11, p.90, p.94
National Council of the Churches of
  Christ in the U.S.A., 18
National Defense Education Act, p.vii
*National Directory of Safety Films,
  1969–1970,* 111
National Education Association, 7, 10,
  52, p.77, p.82, p.92, p.93
National Electrical Manufacturers
  Association, p.93
*A National Guide to the Choice of
  Audiovisual Titles for Use in the
  Study of Modern Communications,*
  see *JEA Media Guide*
National Information Center for
  Educational Media, p.ix, 92, 93,
  94, 95
National Institute of Mental
  Health, p.93

National Instructional Television
  Center, p.86
National Instructional Television
  Library Project, p.93
National Library of Medicine, 43, 54
National Medical Audiovisual Center,
  54, 106, 107, 112, 131, 134, p.90
*National Medical Audiovisual Center
  Catalog,* 112
National Metal Trades Association,
  p.91
National Oceanographic Data
  Center, 73
National Retail Merchants
  Association, 125
National Safety Council, 111
National Society for Programmed
  Instruction, 119, p.79, p.87
National Tape Recording Catalog, p.93
Natural resources, 4, 59, 142
Nature, 61, 62, 64, 103
Nebraska State Department of
  Education, p.94
Negro art, 20
Negro literature, 21
Negro music, 21
Negro poetry, 21
Negroes, 20, 21, 47, 83, 144
*NEMA Movie Guide to 16mm Films
  of Electrical Significance,* p.93
Nervous system, 24, 54, 105, 112, 121
*Neurological and Sensory Disease
  Film Guide, 1966,* 113
Neurology, see Nervous system
Neurosurgery, 105
New Educational Materials, 114
New Mexico Research Library of
  the Southwest, 60
New York Library Association,
  Children's and Young Adult
  Services Section, 62, 67, 123
New York State Education Department,
  56, 96, p.90
Newsfoto Publishing Co., 98
Newsletter, p. 86
*Newsletter of the University Film
  Association,* p.80
Newton, Henry, 83
NICEM, *see* National Information
  Center for Educational Media
Nigeria, 3
99+ Films on Drugs, 115

NIT Newsletter, p.86
Noise, 85
North American Publishing Co., p.81
North Atlantic Treaty Organization
  (NATO), 74
Northeastern University, 118
Norwegian language, 108
Nose, 113
Notes, p.86
Now Available, p.87
NSPI, *see* National Society for
  Programmed Instruction
NSPI Journal, p.80, p.87
Nuclear energy, *see* Atomic energy
Nuclear explosives, 145
Nuclear weapons, 145
Nurses and nursing, 43, 105
Nursing, 112, 121
Nursing education, 26
Nutrition, 37, 54, 121, 130, 141
Nutrition of children, *see* Children—
  Care and hygiene

Obstetrics, 43, 105, 121
Occupational guidance, 134
Occupational therapy, 24
Occupations, 52, 71, 85, 87, 110
Ocean, 45
Ocean life, *see* Marine biology
Oceanography, 73, 87
O'Connor, Thomas, p.92
*OEO Film Guide, Films for Fighting
  War on Poverty,* p.93
Office machines, 150
Office management, 96, 125
Office of Education, 25, 148, p.93
Office practice, 150
Office procedures, *see* Office
  management
O'Hare Books, p.91
Ohio State University, p.85
Ohio University, p.86
Oil, *see* Petroleum
Ollmann, Mary J., 108
*100 Selected Films in Economic
  Education,* p.93
Opera, 65, 89, 126
Operetta, 89
Ophthalmology, 43, 105
Opium, 115
Optometry, 85
Oral pathology, 134

Oral surgery, 134
Orchards, *see* Fruit culture
Orchestra, 52, 65
Organization and management, *see*
  Management
Orthodontics, 134
Otorhinolaryngology, 105
*Our American Heritage: Audio-Visual
  Materials Grades K–14,* 116
Outer space—Exploration, 57, 110
Overhead Transparencies, see *Index
  to Overhead Transparencies*
Overhead transparencies, *see*
  Transparencies
Overweight, *see* Weight control

Painting, 56, 110
Paper, 59
Parent-teacher relationships, *see*
  Home and school
Parker, David L., 55
Parks, National, 3
Pathology, 105
Patriotic songs, 123
Peace, 18, 74
Pediatrics, 105
Pennsylvania State University, 45, 120
Periodontia, 134
Perry, Lucy C., 121
Personal guidance, *see* Counseling
Personality, 36, 68
Personnel management, 66, 96, 125
Personnel service in education, 14, 36
Pesticides, 53
Petroleum, 85
Pets, 61, 62, 64
Pflaum, George A., 103, 144, p.86
Pharmacology, *see* Drugs
Philosophy, 12, 26, 32, 34, 35, 40, 41,
  42, 44, 46, 50, 86, 91, 92, 93, 94,
  95, 99, 100, 101, 102, 110, 114, 118,
  119, 133, 147, 148
Phonodiscs, 12, 40, 102, 126, 140
Phonotapes, 12, 40, 89, 110, 126
Photography, 59, 85, 110
Physical education, 22, 33, 48
Physical education and training, 12,
  32, 34, 35, 40, 41, 42, 44, 46, 50, 86,
  92, 93, 94, 95, 99, 100, 101, 110, 114,
  119, 121, 133, 147, 148
Physical fitness, 112
Physical health, 18

Physical therapy, 105
Physical training, *see* Physical
    education and training
Physically handicapped, 132
Physics, 12, 32, 34, 35, 38, 40, 41, 42,
    44, 46, 48, 50, 73, 85, 86, 91, 92,
    93, 94, 95, 99, 100, 101, 110, 114,
    119, 133, 146, 147, 148
Physiological factors in behavior, 68
Physiology, 45, 105, 112, 117, 121, 130
Pike, Arthur H., 79
Pilkington, T. L., p.93
Plant diseases, 59
Plants, 141
Plastics, 53
Play, 132
Plumbing, 85
Plywood, 59
Poetry, 15, 123
Police Film Guide, 117
Police Research Associates, 117
Polish language, 108
Political science, 72, 83, 91, 110,
    116, 142
Pollution, 149
Pollution of air, *see* Air—Pollution
Pollution of water, *see* Water
    —Pollution
Popular music, *see* Music
Portuguese language, 108
Pottery, 56, 69
Poultry, 141
Poverty, 103, 129, 144
Power reactors, 145
Pregnancy, 130
Preservation of forests, *see*
    Natural resources
Prevention of accidents, *see*
    Accidents—Prevention
Prevention of fire, *see* Fire prevention
Preview, p.87
Prices, 142
Printing, 69, 85, 110
Production, *see* Economics; Industry
Professional Education of Teachers,
    see Annotated Bibliography on
    the *Professional Education*
    of Teachers
Program Planner #4—Biography on
    the 16mm Screen, p.93
Programed instruction, 9, 91

Programed instruction materials, 46,
    91, 118, 119
Programed materials, 90
Programmed Instruction Guide, 118
Programmed Instruction Materials,
    1964–65, p.94
Programmed Learning: A Bibliography
    of Programs and Presentation
    Devices, 119
Propaganda, 74
Psychiatry, 43, 54, 105, 112, 120, 121
Psychodynamics, 68
Psychological Cinema Register: Films
    in the Behavioral Sciences
    Catalog, 120
Psychology, 12, 26, 32, 34, 35, 40, 41,
    42, 43, 44, 46, 48, 50, 68, 86, 91,
    92, 93, 94, 95, 99, 100, 101, 105,
    110, 112, 114, 119, 120, 121,
    133, 147, 148, *see also* Motivation
    (Psychology)
Psychopathology, 68
Psychopharmacology, 68
Public health, 27, 37, 43
Public Health Service, 43, 113, p.91
Public meetings, 66
Public relations, 1, 51, 105
Public Relations Society of America,
    Inc., p.91
Public welfare, 70
Puppets and puppet plays, 61, 62, 69
Purcell, William L., 80

A Quick Reference List of Recent
    Films Adaptable to the Teaching
    of Nursing Subjects, 121

Race discrimination, *see*
    Discrimination
Race problems, 28, 70, 117
Radioisotopes, 145
Radiology, 43, 105, 112, 121, 134
Railroad Film Directory, 122
Railroads, 31, 85, 122
Raimist, Roger J., p.92
Reading, 91, 138
Real estate, 109
Recorded Instruction for Television,
    see *Catalog of Recorded Instruction*
    for Television
Recordings, *see* Phonodiscs;
    Phonotapes

Recordings for Children: A Selected List, 123

Recordings in the Language Arts, see An Annotated List of Recordings in the Language Arts

Records, *see* Phonodiscs; Phonotapes

Recreation, 12, 22, 23, 32, 34, 35, 40, 41, 42, 44, 46, 50, 86, 88, 92, 93, 94, 95, 99, 100, 101, 102, 110, 114, 119, 132, 133, 147, 148

Recruiting of employees, 66

References on Foreign Languages in the Elementary School, 124

Refrigeration, 85

Rehabilitation, 43, 91, 107, 112, 121

Reid, Seerley, 148

Religion, 12, 22, 27, 32, 34, 35, 40, 41, 42, 44, 46, 50, 86, 92, 93, 94, 95, 99, 100, 101, 102, 103, 110, 114, 118, 119, 123, 133, 140, 147, 148

Religious music, *see* Music

Remer, Ilo, p.93

Renner, John W., 38

Research Institute in Communist Strategy and Propaganda, 74

Research Service, p.90

Resources for Learning, p.ix

Resources, Natural, *see* Natural resources

Respiratory diseases, 152

Retail trade, 125

Retail Training Film Directory, 125

Retirement, 66

Revolutions, 5, 39, 74

Rights, Civil, *see* Civil rights

Rivers—Pollution, *see* Water—Pollution

Roach, Helen, 140

Robeck, Mary, 79

Rock music, 126

Rocket flight, *see* Space flight

Rothstein, Jerome A., p.92

Rowman and Littlefield, Inc., 101, 102

Rural development, 70

Russia, 39

Russia, Commun'sm, *see* Communism —Russia

Russia—History, 16

Russia—Social conditions, 16

Russian language, 77, 91, 108, 124

Sacred music, *see* Music

Safety, 111

Safety education, 12, 22, 27, 31, 32, 34, 35, 37, 40, 41, 42, 43, 44, 46, 50, 86, 92, 93, 94, 95, 99, 100, 101, 114, 119, 132, 133, 138, 145, 147, 148

Safety Films, see A Directory of Safety Films

Safety measures, *see* Accidents—Prevention

Sales and Marketing Executives—International, 51

Sales training, 125

Salesmanship, 150

Salesmen and salesmanship, 51, 109

Samson, Nelson T., 59

San Diego State College, p.90

Sanitation, 37

Saterstrom, Mary H., 36, 38

Saving, 1

Scarecrow Press, 140

Schizophrenia, 24

Schneider, John M., 68

Schoenfeld, Madalynne, p.viii

Scholastic Teacher, 114

School administration and organization, 90

School Libraries, p.77, p.87

School Library Journal, p.88

Schools, 111

Schreiber, Morris, 11

W. Schwann, Inc., 126

Schwann Record and Tape Guide, 126

Science, 4, 22, 25, 26, 27, 33, 43, 48, 67, 84, 91, 92, 93, 94, 95, 110, 118, 123, 138, 144

Scottish language, 140

Sculpture, 4, 56, 69, 110

Sea, *see* Ocean

Segregation, 83

Selected Audio-Visual Aids for Traffic Engineers, 127

A Selected Bibliography of Books, Films, and other Materials for Promoting an Understanding of Africa among Young Adults, see African Encounter

A Selected Discography of Solo Song, 128

Selected Drug Abuse Education Films, 129

Selected Films and Filmstrips on

Food and Nutrition, 130

*Selected Films for Migrant
Workers,* p.94

*Selected Films: Heart Disease,
Cancer, and Stroke,* 131

Selected Films on Child Life, 132

*Selected Free Materials for Classroom
Teachers,* 133

*Selected List of Audiovisuals:
Dentistry,* 134

*A Selected List of Recorded Musical
Scores from Radio, Television
and Motion Pictures,* 135

*A Selected List of 16mm Films Useful
in the Field of Librarianship,* see
Films and Librarians

Selected Mental Health Films, p.94

*Selected References on Aging: Films
on Aging,* p.94

*A Selective Discography of Afro-
American on Audio Discs,* see
The Black Record

Self-discovery, 144

Selling, *see* Salesmen and
salesmanship

Senility, 24

Sensory diseases, 113

Serina Press, 82, 83, 84, 85, 86, 87, 88

Service Supplements, p.78

Sex, 68, 103, 144

Sex education, 18, 22, 37, 132, 136

*Sex Education Resource Unit—
Grades K, 1, 2, 3, 4,* 136

Shakespeare, William, 11, 123

Shelter, Donald J., 52

Short Films for Discussion, see
Themes

Shorthand, 96, 150

Sightlines, p.78, p.88

Simmons, Beatrice S., 60

16mm Educational Films, see *Index
to 16mm Educational Films*

16mm Film Catalog: Popular Level,
p.94

*16mm Film Catalog: Professional
Level,* p.94

Slide films, *see* Filmstrips

Slides and Filmstrips on Art, 137

Smoking, 152

Social guidance, *see* Counseling

Social problems, 7, 18, 70, 91, 103,
121

Social responsibility, 144

Social sciences, 4, 11, 12, 22, 25, 26,
32, 33, 34, 35, 39, 40, 41, 42, 44, 46,
48, 50, 67, 83, 86, 91, 92, 93, 94,
95, 99, 100, 101, 102, 110, 114, 118,
119, 133, 138, 144, 147, 148

Social security, 66

Social studies, *see* Geography;
History; Social sciences

Socially handicapped, 7

Society of Data Educators, 79

Society of Motion Picture and
Television Engineers, p.85

Sociological factors in behavior, 68

Sociology, 26, 48, 110

Soil conservation, 141

Solomon, Martin B., Jr., 8

*Sources of Free and Inexpensive
Educational Materials,* 138

*Sources of Information about Newer
Educational Media for Elementary
and Secondary Education,* p.vii

Sources of Teaching Materials, p.viii

Southeast Asia Treaty Organization
(SEATO), 74

South-Western Publishing Co., 150

Space exploration, 139

Space flight, 57

Space sciences, 85

*Space Sciences Educational Media
Resources: A Guide for Junior
High School Teachers,* 139

Spanish language, 9, 77, 91, 108, 124

Speech, 11, 91, 112, 121, 132

Speech disorders, 113

Speech therapy, 24

Speed, William, p.79

Spehr, Paul C., 29

Spelling, 91

*Spoken Poetry on Records and Tapes:
An Index of Currently Available
Recordings,* p.94

Spoken Records, 140

Sports, 25, 27, 33, 37, 84, 87, 88

Stahl, Dorothy, 128

*Standards for School Media
Programs,* p.76

Stanford University, p.viii, 47, p.87

State Department, p.92

State Films on Agriculture, 141

State Loan Film (16mm), see *Guide
to State-Loan Film (16mm)*

Statistics, 91
Steph, Joe E., 36
Stephen F. Austin State College, 59
Stereo-Review, p.88
Sterling Institute, 91
Stevens, Warren D., 3
Stock market, 1
Stories, *see* Children's literature;
    Fairy tales; Legends
Strasheim, Lorraine A., 9
Strip films, *see* Filmstrips
*Study Materials for Economic
    Education in the Schools,* 142
Submarines, 87
Suffrage, 28
*Suggested Series of Movies for a
    Course in Urban Planning,* 143
Suicide, 24
Suites, 135
Supervisory training, *see* Personnel
    management
Surgery, 43, 54, 105, 112, 121
Suttles, Patricia H., 39
Swedish language, 108
Synthetic materials, 85
Syracuse University, 19, p.93
Systems engineering, 13, 91

Teacher education, 10, 33, 104, 150
Teachers College Press, p.94
Teachers Guides to Television, p.88
*A Teacher's Handbook of Resources
    for the Teaching of Health in the
    Secondary Schools,* p.94
Teacher's Record Catalog, p.94
Teaching, 7, 9, 10, 52, 130
*Teaching Aids in the English
    Language Arts: An Annotated and
    Critical List,* p.94
Technology, 19, 27, 45, 48, 98, 118, 144
Technology, Medical, 43
Teenage, *see* Adolescents
Television, 27
C. S. Tepfer Publishing Co., p.84
Textiles, 125
Theater, 15
*Themes—Short Films for
    Discussion,* 144
Therapy, 24
35mm Educational Filmstrips, see
    *Index to 35mm Educational
    Filmstrips*

Timber, *see* Lumber and lumbering;
    Trees
Tobacco, 152
Top of the News, p.77, p.66
Toxicology, 112, 121
Trade, *see* Business
Trades, *see* Occupations
Traffic regulations, 31, 72, 111,
    119, 127
Transparencies, 93
Transportation, 96, 111, 127, 138, 149
Transportation, Highway, 127
Travel, 27, 84, 88
Trees, 59
Trinity University, p.79
Tuberculosis, 152
Typewriting, 96, 150

UNESCO, *see* United Nations
    Educational, Scientific and
    Cultural Organization
UNESCO Publications Center, 65
United Business Publications, p.81
United Nations, 18, 39, 74, 81
United Nations Educational, Scientific,
    and Cultural Organization
    (UNESCO), 18
U.S. Atomic Energy Commission, 145,
    146, p.94
*United States Atomic Energy
    Commission Combined 16mm
    Film Catalog,* 145
*U.S. Atomic Energy Commission
    16mm Classroom Films on Nuclear
    Science,* 146
U.S. Constitution, 39, 72
U.S. Constitution—Amendments, 28
U.S. Department of Agriculture, 141
U.S. Department of Health, Education,
    and Welfare, 25, 54, 78, 113, 124,
    132, 148, 152, p.91, p.93, p.94
U.S. Department of Housing and
    Urban Development, 149
U.S. Department of Labor, p.92
*U.S. Government Films: A Catalog of
    Motion Pictures and Filmstrips
    for Sale by the National Audiovisual
    Center,* 147
*U.S. Government Films for Public
    Educational Use—1963,* 148
United States—History, 11, 20, 29,
    39, 87, 116

U.S. Library of Congress, 75, p.91,
    p.93
U.S. National Commission for
    UNESCO, p.92
U.S. Office of Education, p.vii, 124
United States—Political science, 39
U.S. Public Health Service, 152
University Council for Educational
    Administration, 90
University Film Association, p.80
University Film Foundation, p.80
University of California, Berkeley, 115
University of Colorado, 110
University of Illinois Graduate School
    of Library Science, 153
University of Kentucky Press, 8
University of Michigan, p.87
University of Minnesota, 6
University of Nebraska, 26, p.86
University of Nebraska College of
    Medicine, 43
University of North Carolina, 139
University of Oklahoma Medical
    Center, 68
University of Southern California, 74,
    92, 93, 94, 95, 115
University of the State of New York,
    56, 96, p.90
University of Wisconsin, 91
Uranium, 145
*Urban Outlook: A Selected
    Bibliography of Films, Filmstrips,
    Slides and Audiotapes,* 149
Urban planning, 109
Urban renewal, 71, 109, 129, 143,
    149
Urology, 105
Using Films, p.78
U.S.S.R., *see* Russia

Vegetable gardening, 141
Vegetable kingdom, *see* Botany
Vertebrates, 45
Veterinary medicine, 54, 112
Videotapes, *see* Kinescopes and
    videotapes
Viet, Richard F., 80
Vietnam, 87
*Visual Aids for Business and
    Economic Education,* 150
Visual instruction, *see* Audiovisual
    education

Vocal music, 89
Vocational education, 22, 26, 33,
    71, 110
Vocational guidance, 7, 14, 36, 53, 96
Volta Bureau, p.90
Voting, *see* Suffrage

Wachs, William, 51
Wagner, Robert W., 55, p.85
War, 103, 144
Washington, Booker T., 83
Washington University Libraries, 21
Water, 85
Water—Pollution, 151
*Water Pollution: A Selected List of
    Recommended and Related
    Films,* 151
Water safety, 31
Watson, John Blair, p.80
Weather, 87
Weaving, 69
Webb, Willard, p.93
Weber, David O., 115
Weight control, 130
Welding, 85
Welfare, *see* Public welfare
Western Radio and Television
    Association, p.94
Westinghouse Learning Corp., 100
*What's New on Smoking in Print
    and Films,* 152
Wihtol, C. A., p.93
Wild animals, *see* Animals—Habits
    and behavior
Wildlife, 88
Wildlife—Conservation, 3, 39, 61, 141
Williams, Catharine, p.viii
Williams, G. Mennen, 2
H. W. Wilson Co., p.91, p.92
Wisconsin State University, 30
Wiseman, T. Jan, 98
Wistar Institute Library, 80
Wit and humor, 89
Wittich, Walter A., 40
Wolf, G., 45
Woodwork, 69
*A Working Bibliography of
    Commercially Available Audio-
    Visual Materials for the Teaching
    of Library Science,* 153
World Confederation of Organizations
    of the Teaching Profession, p.90

World Federation for Mental Health,
    p.93
World history, 11
World War II, 74, 87
Writing, 69, 85, 98
WRTA: Index, p.94

X-rays, 105

Young Adult Services Division, p.76,
    p.88
Youth, 144

Ziff-Davis Publishing Co., p.88
Zoology, 12, 32, 34, 35, 38, 40, 41, 42,
    44, 45, 46, 50, 54, 86, 92, 93, 94,
    95, 99, 100, 101, 112, 114, 119,
    121, 133, 147, 148